Brainsp●tting

Brainsp●tting

THE REVOLUTIONARY NEW THERAPY
FOR RAPID AND EFFECTIVE CHANGE

DAVID GRAND, PhD

BOULDER, COLORADO

Sounds True, Inc.

Boulder, CO 80306

This work is solely for personal growth and education. It should not be treated as a substitute for professional assistance, therapeutic activities such as psychotherapy or counseling, or medical advice. In the event of physical or mental distress, please consult with appropriate health professionals, and in extreme cases, the emergency room of your local hospital. The application of protocols and information in this book is the choice of each reader, who assumes full responsibility for his or her understandings, interpretations, and results. The author and publisher assume no responsibility for the actions or choices of any reader.

Cover design by Rachael Murray

Cover image © DrHitch

Printed in the United States of America

Library of Congress Cataloging-in-Publication Data

Grand, David.

 Brainspotting : the revolutionary new therapy for rapid and effective change / David Grand.

 p. cm.

ISBN 978-1-60407-890-9

1. Eye movement desensitization and reprocessing.
2. Psychic trauma--Treatment. I. Title.

RC489.E98G72 2013

612.8'4--dc23

                                  2012037248

Ebook ISBN 978-1-60407-943-2

10 9

To my mother, who taught me to love words.

Contents

Introduction

In 2003, when I discovered Brainspotting, I wasn't looking for a new therapy, at least not consciously. The discovery just happened, or so it seemed. Until that time, I had been successfully using other theorists' methods. I was originally trained in the early 1980s as a psychoanalytic psychotherapist at the Society for Psychoanalytic Study and Research on Long Island, New York, where I live. In 1993, I was trained in EMDR (eye movement desensitization and reprocessing), a more procedural brain-body technique. In 1999, I was exposed to somatic experiencing (SE), which is a deeply body-oriented method. I integrated psychoanalysis, EMDR, and SE into what I called Natural Flow EMDR, a therapeutic method that drew from all three approaches. I wrote about my integrative method in my first book, *Emotional Healing at Warp Speed*, which was released eleven days before the attack on the World Trade Center on September 11, 2001.

Within weeks of 9/11, I was working with a steady flow of survivors of the attack. Over the course of the next year and a half, I did trauma therapy with over one hundred 9/11 survivors, including those in and around the Towers, rescue workers, and family members of those murdered by the terrorist act. Looking back, it was not an accident that I discovered Brainspotting a year and half after September 11. My 9/11 work exposed me, with great intensity, to how humans can be collectively and individually affected by unusual, overwhelming, horrific events. I was forced to relive the experience, over and over again, from so many angles and perspectives. It felt like the exposure altered me down to a molecular level, as happens to those situated too close to a concussive blast. By the summer of 2002, I was truly burnt out, and I was the last to know. In looking for my own healing, I came up with a creative solution to my dilemma: I wrote a play about my experiences and called it *I Witness.*

By standing as witness to the horrors of so many for such a concentrated period of time, my already attuned powers of observation were honed much further. Both consciously and unconsciously, I learned to observe clients' physical cues so acutely that at times it almost seemed like I knew what was coming before it happened. In that heightened state of tuned-in preparedness, I discovered Brainspotting.

The ten years from the birth of Brainspotting to the writing of this book have changed my life. These ten years have also changed the lives of the 6,000 therapists from around the world who have been trained in Brainspotting, and who now see remarkable healing taking place in front of their eyes on a daily basis. But these ten years have mostly changed the lives of countless Brainspotting clients, who have received deep, rapid healing.

Brainspotting is one of the increasing number of what are known as brain-based therapies, treatments that go beyond the mind to gain direct access to the brain. These brain-based therapies are a phenomenon of the last ten to twenty years. Historically, most psychotherapies have fallen into the category of talk therapy, a form of therapy that can be traced all the way back to Sigmund Freud's psychoanalysis (referred to as "the talking cure"). A majority of psychotherapies practiced currently are variants of talk therapy. These treatments are highly diverse, well developed, and generally effective. Most of these approaches are relationally based and require that the therapist be highly attuned to the client. (In psychotherapy speak, there must be a high level of relational attunement, meaning therapists must pay close attention not only to the clients, but also to the dynamics of the relationship between themselves and the client, which mirrors and reveals the client's experience with the primary caretakers of their childhood, especially their mother.) The problem is, and has been, that most talk-based therapies tend to be unfocused, and it takes many months or years of sessions for relief and change to occur.

Most technical therapies, including EMDR, place primary emphasis on the procedures the client has to follow. These procedures are technical and not relational because they require the therapist to lead the client through specifically outlined steps. The degree of attention to technique draws attention away from the essence of the relationship between client and therapist. As effective as EMDR is, by using it, the therapist's attuned relationship with the client does not receive enough attention.

By contrast, Brainspotting is built on a model where the therapist simultaneously attunes to the client and the client's brain processes. With Brainspotting, neither the relational attunement nor the attunement to the client's brain-body processes needs to be sacrificed for the other. In fact, when the two attunements are interwoven together, the healing process is far more powerful and lasting. Since I was a relationally attuned talk therapist long before I was introduced to brain-based models of therapy, it is perhaps no surprise that Brainspotting combines the attunements of both types of therapy. Chapter 6 explores in detail how this "dual attunement" works in Brainspotting and how it makes Brainspotting so effective.

The motto of Brainspotting is, "Where you look affects how you feel." If something is bothering you, how you feel about it will literally change depending on whether you look off to your right or to your left. Our eyes and brains are intricately woven together, and vision is the primary way that we, as humans, orient ourselves to our environment. Signals sent from our eyes are deeply processed in the brain. The brain then reflexively and intuitively redirects where we look, moment to moment. The brain is an incredible processing machine that digests and organizes everything we experience. But trauma can overwhelm the brain's processing capacity, leaving behind pieces of the trauma, frozen in an unprocessed state. Brainspotting uses our field of vision to find where we are holding these traumas in our brain. Just as the eyes naturally scan the outside environment for information, they can also be used to scan our inside environments—our brains—for information. Brainspotting uses the visual field to turn the "scanner" back on itself and guide the brain to find lost internal information. By keeping the gaze focused on a specific external spot, we maintain the brain's focus on the specific internal spot where trauma is stored, in order to promote the deep processing that leads to the trauma's release and resolution.

In my initial discovery of Brainspotting, which I'll share in Chapter 1, my client's gaze locked at a specific position in her field of vision. I knew it did because I saw a powerful eye reflex emerge when her eyes found that position. In this way, her deeper brain was signaling to me that something was locked up inside there. As my client's gaze stayed at that place, she went deeper and deeper into that inner vault where countless traumas were held. Finding this Brainspot unlocked what a year of effective Natural Flow EMDR had not.

In the ten years since that initial discovery, I have developed a wide variety of ways to explore and harness the visual field to unlock and release not only traumas, but also a wide spectrum of psychological and physical symptoms. Each chapter of this book describes a different aspect of Brainspotting, including its different models and how it can be applied.

Chapter 2 describes how our psychology is expressed by the deepest parts of our brains and our bodies: our reflexes. It also outlines the set-up processes that are the foundation for all models of Brainspotting. In Chapter 3, I tell how I discovered that eye positions correlate to our own internal body experience and how that discovery led to two new uses of Brainspotting.

Brainspotting can be used with clients who need to remain grounded during the treatment process, including clients with complex post-traumatic stress disorder (PTSD) and those who are significantly detached from their own experience (those with high levels of dissociation). Chapter 4 explains how a colleague and I discovered and developed a specific model of Brainspotting that could be used with these clients.

Chapter 5 introduces Gazespotting, a variation of Brainspotting that harnesses our natural tendency of gazing at particular eye positions when we think or when we speak—in other words, our ability to spontaneously and intuitively locate our own Brainspots.

Chapter 6 addresses the core of Brainspotting's unique synthesis of relational therapy with direct access to the brain through the visual field. This Dual Attunement Model frames the client's experience with Brainspotting and supports the client's internal healing simultaneously as a human and a neurobiological being.

Unlike many psychotherapeutic methods, Brainspotting is uniquely designed to be integrated into other approaches. The human brain-body system is vast and complex and needs to be perceived and responded to in its individuality. No one technique, including Brainspotting, can address every client situation in its entirety. Chapter 7 describes how therapists are encouraged to utilize the methods they bring to Brainspotting trainings to deepen and enrich their use of Brainspotting.

In Chapter 8, I show you a specific model of Brainspotting called Z-Axis Brainspotting, which can help stuck clients and those having trouble with the process begin to respond and heal effectively.

Chapter 9 examines the centrality of the brain in the Brainspotting process. As noted earlier, the brain is the ultimate scanner, monitoring every cell in the body, as well as itself, on a 24/7 basis. Brainspotting harnesses this scanning ability and the brain's ability to process and heal itself. This chapter also explores Brainspotting as a brain-wise therapy, where the thinking, observing brain can be educated, thereby supporting the healing process.

Chapter 10 addresses how Brainspotting can be used to reduce pain and other physical manifestations. Injuries are simultaneous physical and psychological traumas to the nervous system that become inexorably intertwined. Brainspotting's ability to help unravel the bindings of physical and emotional injuries has implications for treating conditions such as fibromyalgia, chronic fatigue, whiplash, and head injuries. It also makes Brainspotting an effective treatment for combat veterans, who frequently suffer combinations of PTSD and traumatic brain injuries (TBIs).

Brainspotting is an unusually powerful tool for identifying and releasing all forms of sports traumas. Chapter 11 shows how it can be used to help people overcome traumas stemming from sports injuries, failures, and humiliations, all of which accumulate in an athlete's nervous system. This chapter also introduces the Expansion Model of Brainspotting, which can help all athletes, from amateurs to top professionals, perform at dramatically higher levels.

The healing process of Brainspotting is a creative one, and Brainspotting can unleash and expand creativity in artists. Because it works simultaneously with the right brain and the left brain, it both mirrors and integrates the neural art and science. Chapter 12 shows how Brainspotting's various models can be used to help creative people and to inform therapists who work creatively with their clients.

Chapter 13 addresses a variety of ways that anyone can use Brainspotting techniques outside of the therapist's office for relaxation, sleep enhancement, and performance and creativity expansion.

Finally, Chapter 14 tells the story of how Brainspotting became an international phenomenon. Brainspotting is a therapy that is highly adaptable and can be attuned to culture and language. I've trained therapists in South America, Europe, Middle East, and Australia, and the Brainspotting model has also been translated into six languages by eighteen international trainers from three continents.

Although this book is written for the general public, therapists and other professionals will find it highly informative and valuable to their practices. Reading this book, you will learn how profound change is possible, even if you have suffered deeply for many years.

Simply understanding that "where you look affects how you feel" will heighten your self-observation and awareness. The case examples throughout the book will bring you into my office and provide you with a sense of how Brainspotting works and who it works for. The confidentiality of the clients in their stories is protected, as I have changed and disguised key identifying features. You will likely relate to a number of these clients, and hopefully, be encouraged and inspired by their healing stories.

As I am writing, right at this moment, Brainspotting continues to evolve. Brainspotting also is increasingly more available, and many new Brainspotting therapists are being trained all the time. There are resources at the end of the book that will help you locate a Brainspotting therapist in your area.

By following my journey with Brainspotting, you can embark on your own journey. Let reading this book be the beginning of your own Brainspotting experience, wherever it takes you. I offer you the same guidance I share with all of my clients: "Give yourself time and space, and observe your process with openness and curiosity."

CHAPTER 1

The Discovery of Brainspotting

Breakthrough with an Ice Skater

K aren was a competitive ice skater with championship potential. She was a great practice skater, but her performance in meets was subpar. We had worked together for a year of intensive, weekly, ninety-minute sessions. She had come to me with two primary symptoms: during both her precompetition warm-ups and her skating performances, she sensed she was not able to feel her legs, and she felt like she had forgotten her programs.

Karen also had traumatic life history. She was the first-born child in a chaotic family. Her parents fought constantly, so noise and strife surrounded her from infancy. When Karen's sister was born three years later, the family structure split; the girls' mother aligned with Karen's sister, and their father with Karen. This split established a pattern of maternal rejection that carried over into Karen's skating. Her father supported her skating in every way, taking her to myriad practices, lessons, and ultimately competitions. Her mother was uninvolved; she did not attend young Karen's competitions. When her parents' marriage crumbled, Karen was eight, and her mother informed her, "The family broke up because of your skating!"

If that weren't enough to derail her love of and confidence in her skating, Karen suffered numerous injuries on the ice. Skating practice was at least five hours a day, while the competition itself consisted of less than seven minutes—two and a half minutes for what's called a short program and four minutes for a long program. So a skater can put in over a thousand hours of practice for under seven minutes of competition. Accordingly, most injuries happen in practice. In fact, skaters usually fall a number of times during each practice. Although falls and injuries are so common that they're largely ignored, each blow to the ice adds a cumulative jolt to a skater's young body.

Karen was no different than any other skater when it came to injuries; however, when she suffered a physical trauma, a concurrent emotional trauma was lodged in her nervous system along with it. When she seriously injured her back and was taken to the emergency room, she again met the cold blast of her mother's rejection: "It's your fault. This is what you get." It was no wonder Karen would freeze and panic during warm-ups.

The therapeutic approach I was using with Karen was Natural Flow EMDR. Eye movement desensitization and reprocessing (EMDR) is a therapy method discovered in the late 1980s by Francine Shapiro, PhD. EMDR uses left-right eye movements to stimulate the opposite hemispheres of the brain, back and forth. There are hypotheses about how this bilateral brain stimulation works, but no definitive answer has been determined as yet. EMDR's use of bilateral action may help a person to achieve some level of left brain–right brain integration. The left side of the brain controls the right side of the body, and the right side of the brain controls the left side of the body. Our left brain thinks, uses language, and solves problems. Our right brain is intuitive, emotional, and involved in body functions. When we are overwhelmed with emotion and can't think straight, our right brain has taken over. When we are overly analytical and cut off from our emotions, we are stuck in our left brain. But when we are feeling integrated and performing well, our right and left brains are interacting with each other effectively.

To accomplish this left-right stimulation, the EMDR therapist moves their hand back and forth across the client's visual field at eye level, and the client follows the hand with their eyes. This seemingly odd technique appears to strengthen and deepen a person's healing when combined with a set of prescribed steps developed by Shapiro. The first steps include history taking and preparation. Then the therapist has the client retrieve a traumatic memory image and guides the client to think of negative and positive beliefs associated with the image. The client is then guided to bring up the image and the negative belief simultaneously and observe the emotions that emerge. The intensity of these emotions is then numerically rated on a scale called Subjective Units of Disturbance Scale, or SUDS, from zero, the lowest rating, to ten, the highest level. All of these steps serve to stir up, or activate, distress in the client's body.

From there, the rapid left-right eye movements begin. The therapist pauses occasionally to see what's going on inside the client. The internal experience of the client is called processing, and it is actually a focused, powerful form of mindfulness. The client is guided to uncritically observe, step-by-step, what they experience, including memories, thoughts, emotions, or sensations in their body. When the therapist ultimately brings the client back to the original image, to see how it and its emotional charge have changed, hopefully the intensity of the memory has been reduced.

I was trained in EMDR by Dr. Shapiro in 1993 and immediately saw many clients respond to it dramatically. Yet some were too overwhelmed by the power of EMDR, and I needed to modify the procedures. First, I slowed down the eye movements to make them more soothing. Next, I had clients who became too activated shift their awareness from the place in their body where they felt distress to a place where they felt calm and grounded. Finally, I produced

CDs with gentle bilateral nature sounds and music for use during client sessions; these CDs helped clients to feel calmer as they were processing their internal experience. I called my revised version of the therapy Natural Flow EMDR.

I developed Natural Flow EMDR into a workshop that I ultimately taught to other EMDR therapists around the United States and the world. Many therapists who took the training later told me that because of it, they could use EMDR more effectively with all of their clients.

I found that Natural Flow EMDR was especially effective with athletes who often wilt under the spotlight of scrutiny. With her extensive trauma history and severe performance anxiety, Karen found traditional EMDR too overwhelming. With Natural Flow EMDR, she stayed grounded during and after her sessions. With slow, gentle eye movements and an awareness of feeling grounded in the moment, Karen was able to release from her nervous system the traumas of her childhood and her time on the ice.

Athletes are great clients because they approach therapy work as diligently as they approach their sport. Karen had invested herself in Natural Flow EMDR. The results had been excellent. But there was one exception—she still couldn't do a triple loop. This jump was compulsory in one of her two programs, and no matter what we tried, she continued "popping" it, landing after completing only two spins instead of three. This jump was Karen's remaining performance block, and it was a crucial one. Somehow, all of the other techniques that had successfully resolved her inhibition and anxiety in warm-ups and competitions could not break through to her triple loop.

One day, I guided Karen to both see and feel herself doing a triple loop in slow motion, and then freeze the image of the jump at the precise moment she felt herself go off balance. She followed suit and felt a tightening in her torso and legs. Holding the awareness of the tension, I used my Natural Flow approach as she tracked my fingers slowly and gently back and forth across her visual field. Karen reported feeling stuck, but we kept going.

After about a minute, just as my fingers crossed the midline of her nose, her eyes wobbled dramatically and then locked in place. My hand locked along with it. It felt like someone had grabbed my wrist and held it in place!

For the next ten minutes, Karen's eyes remained locked on my unmoving fingers. She watched and reported on a flood of images and body sensations that seemed to come out of nowhere. She watched, wide-eyed, as traumas that had not emerged during her year of intensive therapy now came up and whizzed by. Karen quickly processed through the memories, one by one. She relived sounds and images of family fights, childhood injuries and illnesses, and the death of a grandmother as they all flashed by and seemed to disappear. But what grabbed my attention most were the memories of Karen's traumas, which I thought had fully resolved. Now they reopened and somehow processed through to a deeper resolution. I had never witnessed anything like this in my twenty-five years of practice.

After ten minutes, the torrent gradually slowed, and the eye lock and wobble disappeared. We resumed the eye movements, and the session seemed to end as all others had. Karen's response was so unexpected and confusing to both of us that neither of us commented on it.

The next morning, Karen called me excitedly from the practice rink to report that she had performed a triple loop, with no problem, over and over again. I knew immediately that something new and different had occurred in the session the previous day. I wondered if I had been witness to a breakthrough that transcended my work with Karen.

With each client that I saw that day, I observed closely as I slowly tracked their eyes across their visual field. Every time I spied an eye anomaly, I halted my hand movement, so they would gaze at my unmoving hand. And then I watched and waited. Virtually every time, the process shifted. With some clients, it deepened, and with others, it accelerated. Some clients didn't seem to notice my change of technique and flowed along with it. Others asked me what I was doing. But all of their feedback was compelling. I heard comments like, "Hey, this feels different," "This feels much deeper," and "I feel it all the way in the back of my head." To my great surprise, this new approach seemed even more effective than the one I had already been using. The integrative approach, Natural Flow EMDR, I had used until that time had been highly successful, so the discovery of something significantly more effective was profound.

That was the beginning of Brainspotting.

• • •

Because I was a senior therapist widely known in my professional community, nearly half of my caseload was comprised of therapists, many of them practitioners of EMDR. So when I tried my new technique with them, it caught their attention. As they experienced both the power and novelty of this eye gaze, they besieged me with questions. "What is this?" "How did you come up with this?" "What kind of results are you getting?"—the questions came at me from every angle. I answered by describing my experience with Karen. Most clinicians tend to be curious and experimental, and my clients who were therapists brought my new technique into their practices and reported back to me. With excitement, they told me about breakthroughs and unexpected shifts, even from their more unresponsive clients.

Meanwhile, I kept using my new method with my own clients. After a month, through my own work and the experiences of many other therapists, I had amassed a great deal of anecdotal evidence of the power and effectiveness of my new approach.

People started to ask me, "What do you call this thing?" and I didn't have an answer. I went through bunches and bunches of potential names, like *Eyegazing, Eyefixation, Brainvision,* and others too embarrassing to mention. Finally, while driving from my Long Island home to my Manhattan office, it popped into my head: *Brainspotting.*

• • •

As the months went on, I increased the use of my new method, as did a growing number of my colleagues. They asked if I was going to develop a Brainspotting training, but I felt doing so would be premature. I was still exploring the variety of client responses I was observing. At the same time, as Brainspotting was focusing clients for greater healing, it was opening up new doors of potential exploration. The technique was simple, but the response was complex. I also discovered that eye wobbles and eye freezes were not the only reflexes that revealed the presence of traumas held deep in the brain; I observed many other reactions when I stopped my hand movement, such as multiple or hard blinks and eye widening or narrowing. Any reflex of the face (or ultimately the body) seemed to manifest when the eyes arrived at a position of relevance. I experimented with stopping my hand when I observed a cough, a deep inhale or exhale, a hard swallow, lip licking, a head tilt, a nostril flare, or a change in facial expression.

Each time, the processing appeared to shift notably. Whatever the client was experiencing changed. Images and memories came more quickly. Emotions and body experience went deeper and moved on more rapidly and easily. Clients also got to observe the process while they were in it. The process was fascinating and still is.

As I looked for the reflexive markers in the client's visual field, I realized the subtlety and deftness required to help them find and hold them in place. It was like a dance of connection and attunement between client and therapist, much more than a mechanical process. Clients would often ask how I knew to stop my hand where I did. When I asked if they had any idea why I'd stopped, they seemed to have no clue—even when it was their own nodding head that had stopped me! I sensed the client's reflexive system was cuing me to something at key points in their field of vision.

• • •

Meanwhile, practicality entered the picture, as it became increasingly hard for me to extend my hand in one place for lengthy periods of time, session after session. I tried many methods of holding up my hand, including propping my elbow on a portable table, but nothing worked well.

The problem was in the back of my mind one day when I visited my mother in the home where I grew up in Elmhurst, Queens. My father had died sixteen years earlier from renal cancer, and my mother had left his desk untouched. As I sat in his desk chair, I stared at his pens, papers, and paper clips. Memories arose of Dad sitting at the desk, preparing for one of his countless speeches on Jewish affairs. He was both a national and international lecturer who had brought my sister and me, along with Mom, to far-flung countries throughout our youth. Mindlessly, I opened his drawers, looking inside, awash in memories. The final drawer was empty save one item—a collapsible silver pointer.

"That's it!" I thought. I slipped the pointer into my shirt pocket. For some reason, before I left, I also decided to take my father's fedora hat, which had been waiting for years on the upper shelf of the coat closet. Ideas filled my head.

In my first session the next day, my client was Stan, a fiftyish man with speaking anxiety that dated back to childhood. He was dreading an upcoming presentation at the company where he was an executive. Stan reflected on his last speech, where he froze and delivered a less-than-stellar performance. That memory, paired with the anticipation, pushed his anxiety level off the charts. His stomach clenched, and his heart pounded.

I took out the pointer, extended it fully, and slowly swept it across his visual field. As I moved the pointer across the left half of his field, all I saw was an unremarkable series of blinks and slight facial changes. When I moved the pointer all the way to Stan's right visual field, he began breathing rapidly and started to choke up. I held the pointer steady, dead center on the reflex-evoking spot, and guided him to mindfully observe his inner process.

A series of memories, of traumas from grade school up to college, rattled out of Stan. He gazed at the pointer like it held a lifetime of failures and humiliations. His physical tension eased for a while, plateaued, and then shot up again. He flinched as he visualized a large hand coming at him from his right. "What the hell?" he blurted out. He then saw a three-year-old boy standing alone in the kitchen and crying. "That's me," he said. Then he heard his mother's voice berating him—"You're a bad boy! Why can't you do anything right?" He saw the boy trying to answer, and his mother shot back, "Enough! Don't you talk back to your mother!" She smacked little Stan across the face, from right to left.

Tears ran down the adult Stan's face. As his eyes were riveted on the tip of the pointer, he watched a running series of early memories—recollections of being terrified by unexpected, explosive verbal and physical abuse from his mother during his father's absence. Gradually the imagery slowed and faded.

I asked him to again reflect on his last work presentation, and he realized it wasn't the failure he had believed. Then I guided him to think ahead to the coming speech. He said, "My fear is still there, but less so. I think I have a shot."

I took the pointer down, and we talked for the final ten minutes of the session. Stan was amazed, as he had never made the connection between his being terrorized by his mother and his fear of speaking as an adult. He found it even more remarkable that he always felt more vulnerable on his right side, where his mother used to hit him. Stan reached his hand to his right cheek and said, "I even felt it on my face."

He finished the session by saying, "Maybe past doesn't have to be prologue."

The rest of the day I used the pointer and realized I had found the comfortable way to help clients find and maintain their eye positions. Clients seemed to be almost mesmerized by the silver tip that had replaced my finger.

Since then, every Brainspotting trainee has received a pointer. It was and is required equipment for every Brainspotter in the United

States and around the world. I never imagined that I would become an international lecturer as my father had been. My father had taken his pointer wherever he traveled around the globe to teach. Now I carry it with me on all my international teaching travels. Thanks, Dad!

CHAPTER 2

Outside Window Brainspotting

Reading the Reflexive Cues

For the first six months after my initial discovery, Brainspotting, as performed by me and the therapists who had learned it from me informally, consisted solely of looking for Brainspots by observing reflexive cues in clients at various eye positions. But as I was scanning clients' visual fields, waiting for their reflexes to show themselves, some clients started to point me in other directions on their own. One would say, "Go back. You missed it," and another would say, "It's to the left."

While I was looking for spots of activation from the outside, they were feeling the activation on the inside. In other words, clients were noticing that they felt more intense sensations emerging from their bodies at various eye positions where I wasn't seeing a reflexive response. I realized there was a second way to ascertain relevant eye positions (or Brainspots), beyond external reflexive cues. A second way of Brainspotting was emerging barely after I discovered the first.

Now armed with two ways of finding Brainspots, I was challenged to give them different names. We all know Shakespeare's quote from

A Midsummer Night's Dream, "The eyes are the window to the soul." I called the original method in which the therapist looked into the client's eyes and saw reflexive cues "Outside Window Brainspotting." The second method, in which the client, looking out from the inside, told me, the therapist, where the relevant eye position was, I called "Inside Window Brainspotting."

This chapter explores the nuances of Outside Window, and Chapter 3 will delve into Inside Window.

● ● ●

The first question most people ask when I introduce them to Outside Window Brainspotting is, "How could reflexes tell you where anything psychological exists?" It's a good question, because reflexes are found in all lower species. In humans, some reflexes are so primitive that they are entirely spinal, not even involving the brainstem. The patellar reflex (knee jerk) is such an example; the stimulus to the knee travels to the ventral horn in the spine, then travels back to the knee, leading to the response of the kick without ever involving the brain. This process is so primitive that it involves only a single synapse of the nervous system.

There are virtually countless reflexes in the human system, and they all are involved one way or the other with our survival. That's why a doctor shines a light in a person's eyes to see if they have a brain injury. Our survival instincts are what get us here and keep us here. They both drive us and shape us. Our withdrawal reflex instantaneously pulls us back from the real and proverbial hot stoves in our environment. Our respiratory reflexes allow oxygen to replenish our cells and carbon dioxide to be released from our bodies. The survival instincts are incredibly powerful, so when therapists look for Outside Window reflex markers or spots, it's as if these spots are revealing themselves from the deep brain-body unconscious, where secrets are held in the brain and perhaps the spine.

Do these responses indicate that the seat of what makes us who we are, what determines our psychological selves, is our baseline reflexes? Aren't we more complex than that? Well, we are members of the animal kingdom, and we actually *are* our bodies. The brain is a body part, albeit an almost infinitely complex one.

The human brain can be divided into a number of different parts, depending on how you look at it. Most of us are familiar with the sideways split between the left (or thinking) brain and the right (or emotional) brain. Many of us are less familiar with the triune (or three-part) brain, which goes from front to back. In the front is the cortical or thinking brain, which is found in all primates, but is most advanced in humans. In the middle is the limbic or emotional brain, which is shared by all mammals. In the back is the hindbrain, which contains the brainstem or the reptilian brain, so named for its primitivity.

This hindbrain transitions directly into the upper spinal column, which connects us to a body system that is both primitive and highly complex. After thirty-seven years as a therapist, I have learned that psychological processes are a beauteous interaction between our inner and outer environments. Our unconscious brain reacts at a speed that our conscious, thinking brain can, at best, only follow, and certainly not lead. Our right hemisphere, unshackled from thought and language, can lead us with its vast, attuned intuitive wisdom. Ignore your right brain at your peril!

So it's not such a stretch to consider that our reflexes, our instincts of survival, are the baseline of who we are, what we are, and what we do. Do you think that a smile or frown or any facial expression is not reflexive in its derivation? Or do you think that a mother gazing into her newborn's eyes as the infant gazes back into hers isn't primal? We are at the beginning of studying these survival phenomena using increasingly sophisticated scans boosted by the analyses of mega-computers. And I believe these same phenomena are also the key to finding and resolving trauma stored in our bodies. When the brain scans itself to reveal where it is holding traumas, these reflexive cues are what tell the brain—and us—that it's found something important.

• • •

Here's how the basic Outside Window Brainspotting process is set up and how it appears to work.

In a Brainspotting session, the therapist inquires what the person wants to work on and then determines if the person is activated around it. Looking for reflexive responses in a person who is activated, or focused, around an issue is different from looking for these responses in one who is not. The brain in a resting state looks very different from one that's active. So for Brainspotting to work, the person needs to be activated.

Activation is a specially chosen word in Brainspotting. Other therapies are more apt to use the words *disturbance* or *distress,* but I prefer *activation* because it is more generic and all-encompassing. It is not unusual, in therapy, to use terms that do not capture the essence of an internal experience. I selected the term *activation* to represent how we perceive either emotions or body sensations. To me, activation is the mirror that reflects what we feel in our brains and our bodies, and is crucial in Brainspotting.

For some people, problems and symptoms come and go, and for others, they are ever-present. If a client suffers with a phobia, a trauma, or a relational problem, they may successfully escape it at times, or they may carry it constantly. You might think that people who go to therapy are stressed out most of the time. But problems not only can cause a person to feel too much (hyper); they can also cause a person to feel too little (hypo). Some people are stuck in the hyper, some are stuck in the hypo, and some flip back and forth between the two. If you've ever seen someone just after a car accident, you may notice how shut down they seem. They're not calm—they're in shock. Another term for this state of being shut down is *dissociation,* which means being completely cut off from your emotions or body feelings. Dissociation is a deeply unconscious survival mechanism that is triggered in the face of overwhelming experience. People who have had repeated life traumas, especially starting in childhood, tend to combine under-reaction with occasional breakdowns and intense emotional outbursts.

If a client isn't already activated around an issue, a Brainspotting therapist will guide them to "go inside and do anything you need to do to activate yourself." The next step is to numerically rate the level of activation. For that, we use the Subjective Units of Disturbance Scale (SUDS), which I've borrowed from EMDR. The scale was developed in 1969 by the renowned behaviorist Joseph Wolpe. As explained in Chapter 1, this scale rates the level of disturbance (in Brainspotting, we say "the level of activation") from ten, which is the highest, down to zero, which is neutral or no activation. The SUDS is used effectively in other approaches to not only assess where the client begins, but also to track their progress through the process until they (hopefully) reach a baseline zero. For many clinicians—especially psychodynamic therapists, who work with less structured processes—a rating scale seems quite odd and even anti-intuitive. But it is a highly valuable tool that engages the computational parts of the brain in the process. It also introduces the concept of full resolution, which is alien in many corners of the psychotherapy world.

After the SUDS level is determined, the Brainspotting therapist goes straight to the somatic processes. *Somatic* simply means "of the body." We don't ask about cognitions, beliefs, or emotions. Why not? Because we are looking to drop the client down into their body-brain, far away from analysis, thought, and even language. What's in the body is in the brain, and what's in the brain is in the body. The body and brain are interconnected and inseparable. Brainspotting therapists see the body experience as a form of brain scan, so as the person attunes to their body, they are also accessing and focusing their brain activity. We ask the client, "Where do you feel the activation in your body now?"

The *now* part is important because we are looking to orient and ground the client in the present moment. The problem is in the moment, and the activation is in the moment, as is the healing process. Whatever the client responds with, we accept without question. Body activation is often felt in the head, throat, chest, heart, stomach, or back. Interestingly, these are all areas loaded with neurons, because these areas house the brain (of course), the spine, and the enteric nervous system—the local nervous system of the digestive system, also known as the "gut brain."

After following the steps of activation, determining the SUDS level, and identifying the somatic (body) experiences, we are ready to find the Brainspot. In Outside Window Brainspotting, the therapist slowly moves the pointer across the person's visual field at eye level, starting at either the left or the right. I call this process "mapping for Brainspots," because we observe the client's eyes, face, and, as much as possible, body. Any reflexive response, whether subtle or pronounced, counts.

Mapping for Brainspots is an inexact science; I have found that while all Brainspots seem to work for healing, some give more direct access to core issues than others. However, I have also found that even faint cues, such as the partial blinks that I call "baby blinks," can be meaningful. Reflexes are myriad, and as I described in Chapter 1, can include squints, eye widening, brow furrowing, head tilting, eyebrow raising, lip biting, lip licking, nostril flaring, facial tics, coughing, sneezing, or swallowing. Poker players call these reflexes "tells," because they can reveal an opponent's attempts to hide a bluff or a strong hand. For therapists, these tells reveal information held in the brain and reflected in the body that can focus the healing process.

Blinking tends to be the most ubiquitous reflex we observe in the eyes. Blinking appears to be more complex than you would think, even though it involves simple neural circuitry. Here's my theory on how blinking might relate to Brainspotting: When we blink, we close our eyes for what seems to be a brief moment. However, aspects of the brain are timeless, and so they experience this shutdown of visual input as a significant pause. This shutdown constitutes a change of brain state where all imagery is internally generated. When the blink ends and the eyes reopen, the visual input resumes, and another brain-state change ensues. All of this happens during one seemingly brief event, which suggests to me that no one blink is insignificant or random. And each one may cue the therapist to the presence of a Brainspot in the visual field of a person who is activated. Something is there, and it emerges when we mindfully stop and patiently wait for it.

Once we identify the reflexive location, or Outside Window Brainspot, we guide the client to mindfully observe their inner process, wherever it goes. We encourage curiosity and openness and discourage expectations. "See what comes next—what comes next and then what follows. Don't try to direct the process, and don't try to focus it or hold it back. Trust your instincts," I often say. Some clients take naturally to this process; others have a learning curve, and getting accustomed with the process may take a while.

I call this form of processing *focused mindfulness* because it brings mindfulness to a person who is activated on numerous levels around an issue. In my estimation, it guides the conscious, thinking, observing brain to follow the activities of the deeper brain. The journey, the focused-mindfulness processing, may include thoughts or conscious memories, or it may be comprised entirely of body sensations that continually shift from one part of the body to another. Sometimes it jumps around rapid fire; other times it may seem to be in slow motion. Whether the information that comes up is understandable or not does not seem to be an issue. This journey is sequential, though why one thing follows another is oftentimes puzzling. It is my guess that we are observing a rapid synaptic, neuroplastic journey down vast, intricate neural pathways. In other words, we are witnessing our own brain healing itself.

How can we know that healing is actually occurring? Because when we return to our starting point—the chosen issue and its SUDS rating—change is almost always evident. Sometimes the shift is subtle, and sometimes it is dramatic. The SUDS rating usually drops—sometimes one notch down, sometimes more. The activation may increase, but that is not a problem. It means things are moving and changing; the veil of dissociation may be lifting. But even if there is no quantitative change, we observe a qualitative shift. Anxiety may have morphed into anger or sadness as one emotional state yields to another. When you challenge the brain, you mobilize it; you change it.

Here is a sample of processing from Stuart, a young man of twenty-five who came to me for help with a panic disorder. We were focusing on his memory of school phobia in kindergarten. The SUDS started at eight, and he felt the activation in his chest and abdomen. The Outside Window Brainspot was off to his left, and it was revealed by intense blinking with a series of hard swallows. He gazed intently at the tip of the pointer.

"I see myself in the corner of the room crying," Stuart said. "The teachers and the other kids are ignoring me. I look lost and confused."

He paused and stared silently at the pointer for sixty seconds.

"Everything went dark. I can't see anything. I am terrified. My belly hurts." He literally held his stomach.

"I hear a wailing sound. It's me in my crib at night. I must be two. No one is coming. I cry and cry." At this point, tears streamed down the adult Stuart's face.

"I used to be afraid of the dark. My mother told me I was a difficult child, afraid of everything, even my own shadow. I've had nightmares all my life, being chased down dark alleys."

Here, Stuart again fell silent, witnessing his processing internally. Then he continued.

"Everything went dark again. I started to feel tightness in my throat. Then I had a memory of when I was in second grade. I hated school and pretended I was sick. My parents used to drag me to school. I was miserable. After a few months I finally adjusted, but I never liked it."

He was silent for two more minutes, still staring at the pointer, before telling me, "I jumped to my first semester of college. I came home every weekend. But by the second semester things were a bit better."

I asked him to go back to where he'd started and see what the activation rating was now. It was a six. He said he felt activated in his body—in his throat, though it was not as tight as before.

Stuart's experience illustrates not only how the focused-mindfulness process goes, but also what kind of outcome ensues. Something about this process led to a decrease of the SUDS level and a shift in and easing of the body tension. After two sessions, we reached a SUDS of zero, and this part of Stuart's issue was resolved, processed through.

But this was not a full resolution. In truth, Stuart suffered from complex post-traumatic stress disorder (PTSD) with multiple traumas in childhood and adolescence. His panic disorder was a more diffuse expression of his trauma symptoms, which included early attachment issues with a mother who was carrying her own history of traumas. Stuart's treatment encompassed six months of weekly sessions. As he continued to process his issues with Brainspotting, he got his panic disorder under control, so it affected him only occasionally. He had healed from most of his traumas.

Outside Window Brainspotting was clearly effective with Stuart, and it works well with most clients. Reflexes are ever-present and easily located in most clients. Compared to other forms of Brainspotting you will learn about in coming chapters, Outside Window Brainspotting allows clients and therapists to quickly and easily find and pick up on cues from the deepest parts of the brain and perhaps the spine. However, some clients prefer Inside Window Brainspotting, which you will learn about in the next chapter, because they are more consciously involved in finding the Brainspot.

CHAPTER 3

Inside Window Brainspotting, BioLateral Sound, and One-Eye Brainspotting

Innovations from the Beginning

Brainspotting (later called Outside Window Brainspotting) was an innovation of Natural Flow EMDR, which was an innovation unto itself. Brainspotting by nature is innovative, and I and other therapists trained in my method are always making new innovations to it. Three early innovations in Brainspotting were the Inside Window Brainspotting and One-Eye Brainspotting models, and the incorporation of one of my inventions, BioLateral Sound, into the Brainspotting process. This chapter will explore all three of these developments, starting with Inside Window.

• • •

It has been said that the customer is always right. I believe it is also true that the client is always right. Clients know what they feel from the inside, while therapists, looking in from the outside, are quite limited. So when my clients directed me to Brainspots from the inside while I was searching from the outside, I paid heed. When I look back, it appears obvious that clients would know where Brainspots are by what they feel inside, but honestly, at the time, it was not. In my experience, therapists are taught that they should know how to diagnose and treat clients from outside observation. To a certain degree, they can do so. But the vastness of the neural systems and the uniqueness of each individual make for far less certainty than therapists like to admit.

In this spirit, I have brought the uncertainty principle into Brainspotting, honoring how little we actually know about internal cause and effect. The uncertainty principle actually comes from the work of physicist Werner Heisenberg. In 1927, Heisenberg first published his concepts, and they were a crucial discovery in the early development of quantum theory. In the realm of physics, the uncertainty principle posits that the more precisely one property is measured, the less precisely the other can be controlled, determined, or known. The same applies to human dynamics and what transpires in the therapy office. Most of what goes on inside a person is unknowable, and when therapists intervene in their system, the true outcome is just as unknowable. If this is so, how does a therapist have a clue as to how to intervene?

Once I realized that the human system is so vast as to be unknowable, I surrendered to it. And that surrender was not a defeat—it was a liberation. I no longer tried to know what I couldn't, and instead I began to seek out what I could know, as scant as it was.

In Brainspotting trainings, trainees are taught that any and all Outside Window Brainspots work. I know this is true from my own observations. However, I always wondered what was truly going on, whether subtle or profound, at each Brainspot. I knew that some reflexive responses were more meaningful than others, but could never determine why with any consistency. I wished to have clients hooked up to some machinery that would give me brain-body feedback to make the work more precise. The arrival of Inside Window provided me with that feedback—no brain or body scans required.

Instead, I had the clients' self-observed felt sense to go on. *Felt sense* is a term attributed to therapist and philosopher Eugene Gendlin, who developed a therapeutic method called Focusing, although I have also heard felt sense used in acting classes as well. When clients began directing me to their own Brainspots, telling me, "I feel it more over there," "I tightened up inside," "I felt more anxious over there," and "I just knew," I realized later that this felt sense was coming from reflexes, just like those I was identifying from outside in Outside Window Brainspotting. In other words, the intensification, tightening, or "just knowing" on the inside was also a response to a stimulus, like ice skater Karen's eye wobble and freeze. And the stimulus was also a specific eye position. With some people, the spot was so precise that I kept losing contact with it when I even slightly moved the pointer off the position.

Brainspotting is an observational science; the key to Outside Window Brainspotting is the therapist's ability to closely observe and accurately pick up on clients' reflexive cues. I wondered if Inside Window Brainspotting, which relied on *the clients'* observation skills, would be as effective as Outside Window Brainspotting. My clients and I followed the same first three steps of choosing the issue to work on and making sure that it carried activation, identifying the SUDS level, and locating the body sensations. But then, as the client was slowly scanning horizontally across their field of vision, I instructed them to inform me where *they* felt the most activation, instead of me watching them closely for outward reflexive cues. Sometimes the clients were clear about their felt sense and found a Brainspot on the first try. For others, the felt sense was more subtle, and we had to traverse the visual field back and forth a few times before locating the eye position.

Once we had the Inside Window Brainspot, I observed the client closely to discern any differences between Inside and Outside Window Brainspots—and I have to admit, any difference was hard to determine. Both types of Brainspots both worked extremely effectively, although perhaps differently at times.

Individual preferences were interesting. Some clients liked the conscious control afforded them by Inside Window Brainspotting, while others preferred to turn over the control to the therapist with Outside Window Brainspotting. With some clients, I would use the same method every session; with others, I would alternate between the two. The determination was made by a combination of client preference and my observations of their responses. Sometimes the choice was strategic, and other times it was intuitive. For example, if a client's processing appeared to be genuinely stuck on an Inside Window Brainspot, I might then search the Outside Window Brainspot, and the shift at times jump-started things.

• • •

"The client leads and the therapist follows" was becoming my mantra. And it was leading to innovation after innovation and the ongoing expansion of Brainspotting theory and practice.

Within months of my discovery of Inside Window Brainspotting, another interesting phenomenon occurred. As I was guiding clients' eyes to move horizontally across their visual field at eye level, some started motioning to me to move the pointer up or down. Their directions, "It's up there" or "It's down below," showed me that Brainspots were not located just on the one-dimensional horizontal axis, or x axis. I began to track up and down the vertical axis, or y axis, as well. We now could explore the entire field of vision and not be restricted to a straight line.

With an expanded field of vision, I had to decide how to determine which direction to move the pointer in first. I decided I would first search for the Inside Window Brainspot horizontally at the client's eye level. Once we found a Brainspot on that axis, I would move the pointer first straight up from eye level and then move downward below eye level. I called this first exploring the x axis and then exploring the y axis.

This two-step process was much more challenging than it sounds because finding Inside Window Brainspots could be remarkably precise. Some clients would say, "You missed it—go back" or "You just had it and lost it." Because some clients are less expressive than others, I couldn't always rely on them to report when we'd found the true Brainspot. But when powerful processing followed, resulting in a significant shift in the client's level of activation, I knew we'd found one.

Besides showing me that Inside Window Brainspots could be located along a vertical axis as well as a horizontal one, my clients' feedback also informed me that sometimes it was the movement of the pointer, not the eye position, that was eliciting increased activation. So I divided the search for Inside Window Brainspots into two sectors on the x axis (left or right) followed by two sectors on the y axis (up or down). At each of these four potential Brainspots, I stopped the movement and held the pointer motionless for five to ten seconds. This cessation was to give the client a chance to settle in and assess if the spot was the most activating of all the potential spots.

But I quickly realized that even this method wasn't precise enough, as it ignored the possible spike in activation at the middle of the client's visual field. So I revised the process again: instead of moving the pointer just to the left or right at the client's eye level (the x axis), and then moving it up and down (the y axis), I also stopped at the center point of each axis to see if perhaps that spot held the most activation. I asked the client, "Do you feel the most activation above, at, or below eye level?" pausing at each vertical spot to aid the client's determination of the potential Brainspot. This revised approach for Inside Window Brainspotting is still taught this way around the world.

• • •

In the 1990s, I brought many innovations to the EMDR model, which I eventually integrated into my own modified approach, Natural Flow EMDR. Although this model made use of the power of EMDR, it both softened it and drew from its creativity.

BioLateral Sound was one of my early Natural Flow discoveries. In the early days of EMDR, it was discovered that besides left-right eye movements, there were other ways to stimulate the left and right hemispheres of the brain and so achieve a bilateral effect. One of these was auditory stimulation. The therapist was supposed to snap their fingers close to the client's ears, alternating between the left and the right. This method worked because when we hear with our left ear, the right half of the brain is stimulated, and when we hear with the right ear, the activation shifts to the left brain. Yet this approach always seemed odd to me. I didn't know any EMDR therapist, or anyone else for that matter, who could snap their fingers for more than a minute, let alone an entire session. It seemed to me that more was lost than was gained by this technique.

And yet using sound for left-right stimulation was effective for EMDR processing. It wasn't long before someone developed a sound box with headphones that delivered tones alternately into the client's left and right ears. The speed and volume of the tones could be varied, but the tones were annoying, as was their metronomic quality.

I bought a sound box, tried it out, and was surprised by its effectiveness. Some clients even preferred using it to tracking the left-right eye movements. That was a real eye-opener for me. When a few of my clients had anxiety or depression symptoms that seemed to return soon after they left their sessions, I bought a few extra sound boxes and lent the devices to them for use in between sessions. For some, using the sound boxes made a difference, reducing symptoms in between sessions and increasing the positive effects of the sessions themselves. However, when I encouraged these clients to buy their own sound boxes, all but one balked at spending a hundred dollars for a machine that only produced annoying tones.

I wanted to develop something that would be less costly for clients to buy and more pleasant for them to use. I had already been contemplating how the annoying bilateral tones could be replaced by soothing, healing sounds that moved back and forth from ear to ear. I was wondering if I could come up with a recording that was phase-shifted, or panned left and right in a gentle way.

After months of contemplation, I arranged to go to a sound studio with my friend Evan Seinfeld, lead singer of the heavy metal–rap group Biohazard. We had become fast friends on a flight from New York to Los Anges and shared a mutual interest in healing and sound. So Evan and I traipsed into a studio in downtown Brooklyn, and I emerged ten hours later, at two in the morning, with a cassette in hand. On the drive back to my Long Island home, I popped the cassette into my car player and listened. I liked the original sound, but soon I lost my train of thought. After realizing I had stopped attending to the sound, I focused on it again. Once more I was off in la-la land.

It took me awhile to finally understand what was happening. The tape induced me into such deep processing that I hadn't even noticed it. I thought driving in the middle of the night might have also contributed to my loss of concentration, so the next day I experimented with my wife, Nina, and son, Jonathan. We found that the tape induced processing in both of them as well.

I brought the tape to my office to try it with my clients who were already using the sound box. It worked. Each client preferred it to the sound boxes with the tones, so I introduced the tape to the rest of my EMDR clients. It was a great success with most, except for one or two who simply didn't like the sound. I made inexpensive copies for those using the sound boxes outside of sessions, and they were pleased by both the results and the modest price.

When my clients asked me what I called the sounds on these tapes, I realized that I hadn't thought of a name. In honor of my friend Evan's generous contributions, I combined the name of his group, Biohazard, with *bilateral* and came up with *BioLateral*.

Six months later, I was back in the studio to create four more tracks and record my first CD. I can't resist a joke or a play on words, so I titled my first CD *The Best of BioLateral*. Its success led to demands for more, and over the years I produced seven more CDs, each one more technically advanced and complex than the previous one. I invented a way of moving three different tracks, creating the sound of the ocean depth that felt very dimensional and was perhaps even more healing to the brain than the sound with one moving track. As of this writing, it is now sixteen years later, and I estimate I have sold over 50,000 CDs around the world. Not only did my EMDR clients buy them to use on their own between sessions, but other EMDR therapists also bought them to use with their clients during sessions, replacing the use of eye movements.

When I started using Brainspotting (Outside Window at the time) in earnest, I stopped guiding my clients to use BioLateral Sound in their sessions. I figured that my new paradigm was a different model of therapy, and the CDs, specifically designed for use with EMDR, wouldn't apply. But after a while, a few clients said to me, "I miss the sound. Why can't we use it with the eye work?" I didn't have an answer. But I remembered my mantra, "The client leads and the therapist follows."

When clients put on the headphones and listened to a BioLateral CD while staring at a Brainspot, the Brainspotting process worked even better. The clients were right again. The combination was so effective that I had the rest of my clients listen again to the sound as we did the Brainspotting. Today, not only do I still use BioLateral CDs with Brainspotting, but I also teach other therapists how to do so in Brainspotting trainings. We have clients listen to the sound at a low, almost imperceptible level. At this low volume, the sound serves as a gentle, parasympathetic, or calming bilateral facilitator for most clients. (There are a few clients who are so reactive, sensitive, and/or dissociative that the music is actually overwhelming to them, so we simply have them remove the headphones. These clients also tend to need the Resource Model of Brainspotting, which I will discuss in the next chapter.)

• • •

In 1999, before my first encounter with Brainspots, I was conducting a Natural Flow EMDR training in New York. One of the trainees, Bob Buck, strode up to me during the morning break and said, "David, I have something you will be interested in." He excitedly took out two pairs of electrician's goggles. One pair was painted over completely, except for only the far left side of the goggles, which was left exposed. The other pair was painted in the reverse way, with the far right side left unpainted. I must have given Bob a baffled look as he said to me, "This is going to take some time. Can we have lunch?"

Later, as we sat down together over soup and sandwiches, Bob guided me to put on each pair of goggles, one after the other.

"The light coming from your extreme right goes directly to your left brain," he explained. "And when you switch goggles, the light from the extreme left goes directly to your right brain."

I felt very different with each of the goggles on. With the light coming from the left, I felt emotionally reactive. With the light coming in from the right, I experienced a perspective that felt almost like aloofness.

Bob called these goggles "Schiffer glasses." Harvard psychologist Fredric Schiffer, he told me, theorized that each brain hemisphere almost has a separate personality of its own. For most people, the left brain tends to be more optimistic and the right brain more vulnerable. For about a quarter of the population, the reverse is true. The goggles help isolate these two "personalities" so the therapist can interact with each of them separately. When helping a client process a troubling issue, Schiffer started with the positive side. Then after a while, he guided the client to switch goggles and experience things from the other side. As the client moved back and forth, spending more time on the positive, Schiffer observed that each side began to influence the other. So first you isolate each side, then you effectuate a crossover effect from side to side.

Bob led me through the entire process during our lunch, and it was a powerful and compelling experience. I finished feeling quite calm and balanced. It may have been risky to try out this new process in the middle of a training; it could have thrown off my teaching. But I am an incorrigible experimenter by nature, so I rarely let a novel opportunity slip by me. I went back up to the training room to teach the afternoon part of the seminar and found myself right on point.

At the end of the day, Bob came back to me and said, "Here, David, I made these for you." He handed me two pairs of goggles, painted just like his. I was impressed by his generosity and fervor.

Back in my office, I tried them out again and found the results quite intriguing. The goggles seemed to work just as Bob had described, with some variations. I picked up a copy of Schiffer's book, *Of Two Minds,* and tore through it. Although I saw the value of this method, I found not being able to see my clients' eyes during an EMDR session to be a loss. Additionally, I couldn't use Natural Flow EMDR's slow eye movements because clients wearing the goggles wouldn't be able to track the movement of my hand.

Then I had an idea: what if I painted new goggles where only the left or right half was blocked out? That way, one eye would be blocked but the other would be exposed. I would then be able to use the left-right phenomenon and the eye movements together. I bought two pairs of electrician's goggles and blacked out the right side on one and the left side on the other. Back in the office, I had my first client of the day try them out.

Frank was a police officer struggling with memories of a series of traumatic experiences on the job. Early in his career, his partner was shot and killed during a drug raid. He was now on administrative leave with his gun pulled because he had fired it in a street situation where he felt his life had been threatened. Frank was overwhelmed with roiling feelings, from guilt to anger at being doubted by the superiors he had served loyally.

At my instruction, he put on the goggles, covering his left eye and exposing his right. I had him reenact the street situation and having his gun pulled, and his SUDS level was four. When he switched to the goggles exposing his left eye, the SUDS jumped to eight, and he felt a stabbing pain in his heart. I immediately had him switch back to the other goggles, again exposing his right eye, the "calmer eye." We started slow eye movements. Frank quickly calmed down and gently processed the experience and its consequences.

When he had attained the zero SUDS and no recounting of the incident flared him up, I then had him switch goggles again. With his left eye exposed, the activation he experienced was far more subdued than it was on his first exposure with that eye. As he tracked my finger across his visual field, he offered, "I see it replaying and realize I was justified. I did the best I could. And the same is true for my superiors. Time to move on." Frank was equally calm on both sides of his brain. Splitting the difference of his left and right hemispheres was a clear enhancement. I was impressed.

With the advent of Brainspotting, I placed the goggles aside. Outside Window Brainspotting necessitated observing the clients' full range of vision. But the advent of Inside Window Brainspotting changed the equation.

I was working with Kate, a young woman struggling with years of diffuse anxiety and chronic low-level depression. Nothing seemed to focus her, including Brainspots. My eyes were drawn to the neglected goggles languishing on my desk. "Why not?" crossed my mind. So I asked her to alternatingly try on both pairs.

With the right eye exposed, she told me she felt "not much." When she switched, exposing her left eye, her head recoiled, and tears ran out of her eyes. I picked up my pointer to determine which position on her left eye gave her the most activation. Moving the pointer left and up, I hit the spot, and we were off to the races. Intense processing revealed childhood abandonments and humiliations at home and at school. Kate watched a "highlight reel" of a lifetime of pain and disillusionment. This process continued for many sessions, which left her both enervated and relieved.

Eventually, all was quiet on the western front. I assumed that the deep healing on her vulnerable left eye didn't leave much to do on her right, but I decided to check anyway. When she switched goggles, leaving her right eye exposed, the highlight reel started again. Some events were new, but some were memories that emerged on the left eye—memories we thought had been resolved. It took only two sessions for Kate to attain quiescence.

The left- and right-brain dichotomy had come to Brainspotting. Not only could I Brainspot the entire visual field and neural processes, but now I could also zero in on either hemisphere when increased focus was needed. I called this variation One-Eye Brainspotting. Soon after, I realized I could also use the one-eye approach with Outside Window Brainspotting, when greater focus was needed.

This method allowed for greater specificity in addressing vague, elusive conditions, including those psychological and those physical. Not only did One-Eye Brainspotting apply to anxiety, depression, and detachment, it at times helped reduce symptoms from conditions like chronic fatigue, fibromyalgia, and ADHD (attention deficit hyperactivity disorder). I experimented with One-Eye Brainspotting to see where it made a difference and where it didn't. Some patterns emerged, but some clients seemed to randomly respond better to or prefer One-Eye over the other, two-eye versions and vice versa. One-Eye Brainspotting became a mode to be used when clients seemed to need more focus and/or higher activation.

I called the eye with the higher SUDS level the Activation Eye and the one with lower, the Resource Eye. I observed that you couldn't predict in advance which eye would be more activated than the other. The basic procedure became identifying the Activation Eye and working with it through to a zero SUDS, and then crossing over and processing any remaining activation on the Resource Eye. I noticed that the eye position, or Brainspot, often changed when the client switched eyes. The Brainspot that brought up the greatest activation on the first eye we processed was not always the same location when we crossed over. Somehow, the brain was revealing itself, even though I was uncertain as to how and why.

• • •

Brainspotting is like the proverbial river. You can never step in the same place twice. It is always changing, always evolving. Sometimes I have trouble keeping pace with my own observations and discoveries. This truth applied to One-Eye Brainspotting.

I was working with a client who was so reactive he would get triggered by the drop of a hat. Ted was highly dissociative due to a childhood rife with physical, emotional, and verbal abuse. There may have been sexual molestation in his history, but at the time I tried One-Eye Brainspotting with him, it hadn't emerged yet. The focus of gazing at a Brainspot tends to be containing for clients (meaning they would be more focused and less overwhelmed), but Ted would become overwhelmed with any Brainspot, Inside or Outside Window. Ted had "failed" in previous treatment attempts with many therapists armed with a myriad of techniques. I didn't want to let him down and add my name to his roster.

Again I spied the goggles, and an idea popped into my head: "How might Ted respond if we started him off the Brainspotting on the Resource Eye?" We gave it a whirl.

Ted's activation level was a ten with both eyes open. But when he covered his left eye, his activation dropped to a SUDS level of four. That was clearly his Resource eye. Ted put on the goggles covering his left eye and was able to fruitfully process his traumas for the first time. Mind you, the processing was not quick or easy, but it was doable. And it went on for many sessions. Ted's brain and being had been infiltrated by daily childhood abuse, and his healing was both volatile and circuitous. But he could leave the sessions intact, and afterward he would not suffer his usual nightly terror states while asleep. (During his sessions, I also repeatedly guided Ted to bring his awareness to his Body Resource, a specific place in his body where he felt calm and grounded. Chapter 4 explains the Body Resource and its role in Brainspotting in detail.)

After four months, Ted attained his first zero SUDS level. My curiosity got the best of me. Was Ted ready to switch over to the Activation Eye? Could he handle it? I asked if he wanted to try, and Ted reluctantly agreed. Turns out he understood himself better than I did. ("The client is always right" is a lesson I have learned repeatedly.) He immediately became overwhelmed with panic. I instantly had him switch goggles, and it took him the rest of the session to get his feet back on the ground. I apologized for my overzealousness, and Ted graciously accepted my apology.

But I'd been given another fascinating lesson on the myriad mysteries held by the brain. Trauma will block "the great communicator's" innate capacity to know itself. In time, Ted was able to find his way back to his Activation Eye, his eye of vulnerability, and complete his healing, but it took months. The power of Brainspotting has its limitations. However, the healing that often takes years with other therapeutic approaches can sometimes happen in months with Brainspotting, and decades of therapy can be telescoped down to years.

CHAPTER 4

The Resource Model of Brainspotting

The Brain-Body Is the Ultimate Resource

used to be a major proponent of EMDR. From the moment I was trained and brought it back to my office in 1993, I was able help many clients heal more quickly and effectively than before. It also revealed that my clients were carrying more trauma and dissociation than I knew. An expert therapist became a novice again, but the new opportunity was truly a blessing.

The new information set off a growth spurt in me both professionally and personally. In my book *Emotional Healing at Warp Speed: The Power of EMDR,* I tell the story of how my buddy Uri Bergmann (now a Brainspotting expert) dragged me to the first EMDR training. We quickly became the Batman and Robin of EMDR advocacy, booking presentations wherever we could to spread the word of its unique healing properties. Clinics, hospitals, professional associations—none of them escaped our grasp.

In 2000, I was invited to present EMDR at an AMCHA (which means "our people" in Hebrew) trauma conference in Jerusalem. It was an honor, and I gladly accepted. The opening speech was given by American trauma expert Peter Levine; in it, he talked about somatic experiencing (SE), his approach to treating trauma, which was quite new to me.

Peter showed a video to illustrate the animal's natural response to threats. One clip was of a polar bear being shot with a tranquilizer gun. Immobilized, the unfortunate bear lay on its side. As the sedative wore off, the bear struggled to his feet and started to shake violently. Once this trembling was over, the bear ran off like nothing happened. The bear showed the natural capacity to shake off trauma, a trait that humans have basically lost. Peter went on to say that healing from trauma entails the resolution of the natural brain-body threat response that, in humans, gets frozen in a state of incompletion. Shaking it off is necessary to bring a person out of trauma and return their body to a state of groundedness.

The polar bear called to my mind a few of my clients who had shaken, at times violently, during EMDR processing. I had mistakenly thought this shaking was a problem, when in truth it was essential to their healing. Peter had gotten my attention.

I wasn't going to give my EMDR presentation until a few days later, so I decided to attend his SE workshop. I was sitting in the back, taking it in, when he asked for a volunteer to help demonstrate his method. My hand shot up. I strode to the front of a room of one hundred attendees, and Peter asked what I wanted to work on. I frantically searched for something worthy. My fear of rodents popped into my head. I'm afraid of mice, but I hate rats.

Peter asked me where I was feeling distress in my body, then asked where in my body I felt calm. He guided me to shift my attention to the place of calm, and spontaneously I closed my eyes. My head started moving on its own, and Peter responded by putting one hand gently on the back of my head while the other cradled my neck.

In moments I was traveling down a swirling vortex, asking myself, "What is this?" "Birth canal" was my answer from within.

My entry into this world, I knew, had been eighteen hours of trauma with the umbilical cord wrapped around my neck. With Peter guiding me, I went deeper and deeper into the process. Time and space disappeared, but soon I was slowly coming back to the training room. I felt held and peaceful. I opened my eyes and saw Peter's reassuring face. I looked out to the audience and realized I had forgotten I was in front of roomful of people. I checked out my watch and realized I had been up there for almost an hour. When I arose from the chair, I noticed that my posture was straighter than I could ever remember it being.

At dinner, I sat down at Peter's table, and we discussed the experience he had ushered me through in that afternoon's session. He explained how he had "pendulated" me back and forth between my "healing vortex" and my "trauma vortex." He was careful to keep me in the healing space and only occasionally took me momentarily to the outer edge of the trauma space.

Peter's information was all new to me, but intuitively it made sense. I told Peter I was at the conference to present EMDR, and he reflected that it is very powerful technique—in fact, at times, too powerful. He said that it is retraumatizing for people to get too activated during the healing process. "Slow is fast and fast is slow," he told me, adding, "The body is the ultimate resource." These two ideas stuck in my mind as I headed back home to New York.

• • •

A few months later, I attended the first part of the SE training. Somatic experiencing was very different than EMDR because it emphasized gently tracking body sensations. In the training, we were taught to shift an activated person's attention to the place in their body where they felt calmest and most grounded. We were also instructed to not let the person focus too much on their body's distress. The idea was to only take the person to the outside edge of the tension or pain, and to do so only briefly. The trainer explained how touching this edge helps to unfreeze and discharge the trauma. I was impressed with the method and impressed with the results.

Back in my office, doing my already gentled down version of EMDR, I wondered how to integrate it with SE. The EMDR protocol entails starting with a target image, finding a negative cognition (or belief) associated with it, and then locating a counterbalancing positive belief. The next step is accessing the emotional response and then identifying where the activated distress is held in the body. This is followed by what is called desensitization, which is accomplished with eye movements. The therapist induces the eye movement by having the client track the therapist's fingers as they move back and forth from right to left. As the client moves their eyes, they observe their inner processing.

The thought came to me, "What if, after identifying the body distress, we ask the client to find where they feel calm and grounded in the body?" I named the identified calm, grounded feeling in the body the Body Resource. (I'm not sure if I coined this term or if I had received it from Peter Levine.) I speculated that combining the Body Resource with slow, gentle eye movements might help fragile clients not get overwhelmed and retraumatized, as I had seen some of them do with EMDR. I tried it out and found that this new combination of Natural Flow EMDR and SE was highly effective with clients who were too fragile for the standard EMDR approach. (It should be noted that I purposely did not use the words *safe* or *safety* in connection with the Body Resource, because many people have grown up without safety or had the experience of repeatedly losing it. Finding a place of safety in the body is more unpredictable than one might think.)

I wondered if having less vulnerable clients do their processing through the calm, grounded place would lessen the powerful healing effects I had been observing. I experimented with many clients and found there was no drop-off in the results. In fact, the outcomes were often enhanced.

I added the Body Resource to the EMDR protocol, after the step of locating where a client held distress in their body. This synthesis became one of the cornerstones of Natural Flow EMDR, which I also called Parasympathetic Processing. It was my observation that traumatized people could best heal in a state of parasympathetic deactivation (calming down) as opposed to sympathetic activation (preparing for action). It made sense, because when we are aroused into a survival state, all our brains and bodies can focus on is getting out of the situation intact. In order to heal, we need to be in a calm, grounded place.

A few years later, I gave Peter Levine a brief experience of Natural Flow EMDR with the Body Resource I had borrowed from his SE. He was impressed.

• • •

Early after my discovery of Brainspotting, I actively experimented with combining it with the Body Resource. The result was a variation of Brainspotting that we called the Resource Model, or Resource Brainspotting. With the development of the Resource Model, I had to come up with a more precise name for the Brainspotting we had been doing since the beginning. I decided that the original approach would be called the Activation Model of Brainspotting because we were working with clients in an intentionally elevated state of activation.

I originally observed that gazing at Brainspots was much more containing for clients than the eye movements of EMDR. Holding the eyes still in a gaze creates less brain activity than moving the eyes, especially moving the eyes quickly. I accordingly thought the Body Resource would be needed less in Brainspotting than in Natural Flow EMDR. To some degree that was true. However, Brainspotting is so laser-like that buried traumas can be quickly unearthed. Re-encountering these traumas can be very activating, and for some fragile clients, even destabilizing. When that happened,

I quickly shifted the client away from their awareness of their body activation to the calm, grounded resources of their body experience.

I like to tell my clients that "what's in the body is in the brain, and what's in the brain is in the body." This means that everything, including body sensations, is felt in the brain. Thus, a pain in the knee is actually an illusion, as it is, in truth, a pain from the knee but felt in the brain. If you ever see an fMRI or SPECT scan of the brain of a trauma survivor, the areas of activation are usually represented in yellow or red, because of the increased blood flow in these regions. Areas of calm or quiescence are usually in blue, which reflects normal blood flow. The area of the body where the person feels activated probably correlates to the yellow and red in the brain, and the blue areas are likely where the body's calmness or groundedness is held in the brain. So when Brainspotting therapists guide someone to shift their awareness to their Body Resource, they are actually putting them in touch with their Brain Resource. Moving attention to this place is helpful and relaxing for anyone, but for someone suffering from trauma or other psychological conditions, it can be profound. Accordingly, the Body Resource is the foundation of the Resource Model of Brainspotting.

• • •

The first expansion I made to Brainspotting was to develop the concept of a Resource Brainspot (now called the Resource Spot), based on the idea of the Body Resource. This spot is derived from Inside Window Brainspotting, as the conscious participation of the client is needed to find it. You recall the therapist moves the pointer horizontally first (along the x axis) and vertically second (along the y axis) to find the eye position where the client feels the activation the most. We do the same with the Resource Model, only here we are looking for the spot where the client feels the calmest or most grounded.

Brainspotting is a more containing, focused process than EMDR, with its continuous, fast eye movements. The Body Resource, along with slower eye movements, makes EMDR more gentle and user-friendly for clients. In the more containing model of Brainspotting, the effects of the Body Resource are even more profound. In fact, it is arguable that Brainspotting's Resource Model is so effective that it should be used with all clients. For years, Lisa would encourage, urge, and cajole me to use and teach the Resource Model more than I did. I believed that maintaining the gaze on the eye position was enough for most clients. But Lisa and many of our Brainspotting trainees were working with a more vulnerable, traumatized, activated clientele, and they were using the Resource Model more frequently than I was. The Resource Model is now seen and applied along a spectrum, from the most activated applications of Brainspotting to the most resourced applications, depending on the needs of the client. I call this the "fully articulated Resource Model of Brainspotting," which means that its concepts and techniques can be individualized and used with all potential clients.

• • •

One of the first clients I successfully used the Resource Model with was Fernando, a forty-year-old man who suffered with insomnia and fibromyalgia stemming from a long history of being mercilessly bullied in childhood. He had an unusually shaped head that was narrower from front to back than side to side, the result of a birth anomaly. Because of this distinctive physical characteristic, Fernando had suffered verbal abuse and humiliation that at times led to being pushed and hit. Many girls in his class joined in the taunting. His teachers didn't seem to notice or care, which only made things worse. All this led to a deep sense of inferiority and a deep belief of, "I am not good enough." The hurt and the buried rage festered inside, ultimately leading to body pain and the inability to let go and fall asleep.

Fernando persevered and pursued a professional career, but his suffering was unending. He was afraid to approach young women, convinced he would be rejected once again. He had only few close male friends, believing that people simply can't be trusted.

In his first few sessions, I engaged Fernando gently and wanted to give him a positive Brainspotting experience. Our first trial was with memories of the most egregious of his bullies. His SUDS level was off the charts. He felt anxiety and pain coursing throughout his body when he recalled the worst incidents of his victimization. We started on an activation spot, and I quickly had him locate his Body Resource; in his case, the place where he felt calm and grounded was the place where his feet touched the carpeted floor of my office. Memory upon memory of abuse and humiliation came and went, only to be replaced by another. Gradually, with the ongoing processing and release, the SUDS level dropped.

But Fernando reported intense, disruptive post-session processing and sleep even more disturbed by night terrors. So in the next session, I went right for a Resource Spot, the eye position that gave him the same sense of contact with the present that the feeling of his feet on the floor provided. Interestingly, he felt most calm and grounded when his eyes were fixed in the middle of his visual field, at eye level. This spot was, in essence, the point of eye contact with me. His dark eyes gazed into mine, searching for signs as to whether he could trust me to not reject or humiliate him. Session after session, his eyes probed mine with uncertainty and woundedness. Eventually he was able to perceive the empathy and compassion that resided in my eyes.

It took many months of this processing, and Fernando certainly put my endurance to the test. But finally he was able to stop hearing the taunts that he had internalized, and he heard a voice from inside that said, "You are good enough." Fernando understood that the voice emanated from his core, which knew the truth about him. He began to sleep better and feel a more positive connection with his body. He even gained the confidence to risk asking a young woman out on a date. She must have seen what he had discovered in his core. I am convinced that Fernando's feet planted firmly on the floor of my office and his eyes riveted on mine were necessary for him to heal.

CHAPTER 5

Gazespotting

Where You Look Does *Affect How You Feel*

Have you ever noticed how someone deep in thought can gaze at a spot on the floor for what seems like an eternity? Or have you ever realized you were doing the same thing and wondered, "Why I am I staring at that? It's just a pattern in the carpet." Have you ever watched someone speaking passionately, not to you, as their conversation partner, but to a crack in the ceiling? These observations might strike us as odd and inexplicable, yet they are ubiquitous and compelling. Some believe looking at these "meaningless" spots is a form of avoiding eye contact. It is clearly not, as we can plainly see the person's focus is magnetized on the particular spot.

It is ironic that this phenomenon, which I call Gazespotting, was the third way I discovered to locate relevant eye positions, or Brainspots, because it is the most obvious means of doing so. We all experience this phenomenon all the time. We just don't notice it because it is a product of our unconscious brain. The conscious, thinking brain can't comprehend it, so that part of the brain labels it as odd, random, or irrelevant. But the unconscious brain does understand this phenomenon, because this aspect of the brain engages in it so instinctively.

So while I was exploring the Outside and Inside Windows, I didn't notice the Gazespotting window that opened and closed on its own. When I discovered its power, there was no looking back, so to speak. I realized that this intuitive staring could be a third way of locating Brainspots. It occurred to me that all therapies use Gazespotting, albeit unconsciously. I now know that when I was in psychoanalysis, laying on the couch, my eyes locked every session on a crack in the ceiling, I was drawn to that spot because of the brain access it provided me. I wonder if my analyst would believe me if I told him that now—or then. I believe that all therapies, spanning from psychoanalysis all the way to cognitive behavioral therapy, are focused and enhanced by unrecognized Gazespotting.

Here's how I recognized it. I was working with James, a businessman in his fifties with fear of public speaking. He had a history of shyness and social phobia in his childhood and adolescence. His father was an angry man who impulsively ridiculed and verbally abused his children. He called James and his siblings "dummies," and a common refrain was, "Shut up. You don't know what you're talking about." James's mother did not protect her children. In fact, she too was a recipient of the scorn and was cowed by it herself.

The adult James was intelligent and industrious, and he attended college and attained an MBA. He was successful in the business world, but was held back by the remnants of his social phobia, which manifested as fear of public speaking. Presenting at business meetings, a requirement of his position, felt like facing a firing squad sans the blindfold and cigarette. The worst part was the crippling anticipatory anxiety that preceded any presentation.

James responded well in our sessions, but didn't seem to be able to maintain his gains when back out in the world. I had used a combination of Inside and Outside Window Brainspotting; One-Eye Brainspotting and the Resource Model were also occasionally part of the mix, as was the more challenging Activation Model. During one session, James was beside himself as he thought about an important negotiation session where he had to speak on behalf of his company. As he spoke passionately about his anxiety and nightmares, I suddenly noticed that his eyes were locked on a spot on the floor next to my chair. As I listened to him, I observed that his gaze seemed welded in place. When he finally took a break and reestablished eye contact with me, I had a thought: "What if I have him process off of that spot on the floor, instead of helping him find a spot with the pointer?"

I said, "James, I noticed as you were talking to me you were staring at a spot on the floor right next to my chair." I pointed to it, and his eyes returned and locked back onto it.

I continued, "As you look over there and think about the meeting, how activated do you feel between zero and ten?"

James responded, "Eight," and when I asked him where he felt the activation in his body, he put his hand on his chest and said, "Right here." He was quickly processing, but his memories didn't return to his father's angry diatribes. Instead, he remembered trying to fall asleep, at two or three years of age, while his father screamed at his mother. His father went on and on, mercilessly berating her about what a terrible housewife and mother she was.

"I feel frozen," James croaked, holding his throat. As his eyes stayed locked on the Gazespot, similar memories flashed through. His panic spiked and then abated. After a half an hour, he spontaneously closed his eyes and remained that way for five minutes. When he opened his eyes, he looked directly into my eyes and said nothing. I asked how he felt. He replied, "I think I can do it." His meaning was clear.

The following week James came in, sat down, and said, "It was about 50 percent better. Let's go." His eyes locked back on his Gazespot. This pattern continued for three more sessions, with further gains each time.

Then James arrived at the fourth appointment and started to talk, only this time, he was gazing upward to a spot on the ceiling. This became his new Gazespot, and he quickly had memories of staring up at his father, facing another verbal beatdown. This Gazespot led to fruitful processing, which extended for two more sessions. Afterward, James reported that his speaking anxiety was either gone or contained at such a low level that it didn't bother him. In a few more sessions, he completed his treatment, although he still comes back occasionally for "a tune-up."

After my discovery with James, I couldn't help but pay attention to where my clients looked as they were talking, especially when they were talking about their most powerful, emotionally charged experiences. Some clients locked on one spot; some gazed at two, three, or more. I made mental notes of where they looked the most, where they looked the longest, and where they appeared to be the most activated. The more I experimented, the more I saw interesting results.

And clients took to Gazespotting so naturally, it was like they didn't even notice they were Brainspotting! When I wasn't sure which of their numerous Gazespots to have them focus on, I asked the clients to choose themselves. It seemed they always knew intuitively where to look. Gazespotting became an excellent way to introduce Brainspotting to new clients. They didn't have to be guided to a Brainspot or have the odd experience of staring at the tip of a pointer. Once they saw the power of a Brainspot, it was usually easy for them to understand and transition over to Inside or Outside Window Brainspotting.

In my ongoing experimental zeal, I wondered which type of Brainspotting was the best. Did Gazespotting make the other modes obsolete? I eventually found that all three models were different, and each was unique. Some clients responded best to one type, while others didn't respond to it at all. Some clients had preferences, but their preferences were hard to predict. A number of clients told me that Gazespots, as I called them, were not as powerful as Inside Window activation spots and they felt they didn't get as much out of them. They were more of the "go for it," adventurous types for whom more is better.

• • •

In their study of eye fixation, Susana Martinez-Conde and Stephen L. Macknik (*Scientific American,* August 2007) found that the eyes continue to move imperceptibly when we fix our gaze. These "micro-saccades" are necessary, as completely fixed staring gradually leads the object of our attention to disappear from our vision. Martinez-Conde and Macknik also speculate on, and are studying, the myriad effects in the brain of fixed-eye gaze. Perhaps at some point our paths will cross, and each of us will be able to contribute to the other's experimental work. It is my firm belief that the answers to how and why Brainspotting works are in the brain and its connection to the eyes. I also believe that what we have found out from all our clinical Brainspotting explorations will help scientists better understand the mysteries of the brain.

Because clients appear to have less activation processing on Gazespots than on traditional Brainspots, the question has arisen, "Is a Gazespot a form of a Resource Brainspot?" It is an interesting postulation, and the answers appear subtle and nuanced.

The activation people feel when looking at Gazespots seems less intense than the activation they feel at the Brainspots revealed by Inside or Outside Window Brainspotting, and for most clients, Gazespotting is a gentle process that seems to flow easily. (A few clients have responded to Gazespots with, "I don't want to look there. I don't like how it makes me feel." It was as if their eyes were drawn to an accident on the highway; they were compelled to look even though it felt aversive.) Upon further inspection, Gazespots contain different properties than Resource Brainspots, which are searched for so deliberately and assiduously for their calming, grounding properties. I have observed that clients who are highly dissociative and vulnerable to being overwhelmed do better with the Resource Model. It is clear that they need to have their feet planted firmly in the present by this model. Gazespotting is natural, but not literally or figuratively grounding in the way the Resource Model is.

My sense is that Gazespotting is a process that accesses the brain quite differently than either Inside or Outside Window Brainspotting. It strikes me as a spontaneous way of scanning our inner neural environment by intuitively scanning our visual field. Through unconscious mechanisms that seem to stem from our animal heritage, we know where to look for what we need. This reaction is called the orienting response, and it also involves scanning for danger as well as for safety. It is actually a reflex designed to help us locate the safety of shelter or the presence of food.

But the deep, intent way we gaze, at times for many minutes, reflects how it is helping us access and maintain our focus on something inside. And that process is both experiential and neurally informational. Using our outward gaze gives us something deep inside that we need, even if it is completely out of our unconscious awareness. We are deep in thought as we are deep within ourselves.

Think of the "thousand mile stare" we see in combat veterans and survivors of natural disasters. It's usually perceived as a marker of dissociation, as if the person isn't really there mentally. But things are not always what they appear or what we interpret them to be. In my judgment, the far-off gaze is a reflection of a person looking deep inside themselves, to a far-off place in their unconscious. They are not "gone"; they are just searching for something that is very elusive and far, far away inside. When I have guided these trauma survivors to notice where their eyes are fixating in the room and report back to me on their internal process, memories emerge, and in time, the people "come back" to the present.

When I teach Gazespotting in a Brainspotting training, I offer one caveat: "This model is so natural, simple, and effective you will be tempted to use it exclusively, to the neglect of all your other Brainspotting tools. Don't fall into that trap." Brainspotting is both an art and a science comprised of infinite variables and combinations thereof. It is a reflection of the brain as an organ that has infinite structures and functions that are expressed intuitively. Never underestimate the brain's endless, unquenchable nature to survive and adapt to its environment, both internal and external.

CHAPTER 6

The Dual Attunement Frame

Staying in the Tail of the Comet

The client is like the head of a comet. The role of the therapist is to find their way into the tail of the comet and follow the head wherever it goes. The moment the therapist thinks they know where the comet is going, they fall out of the tail. "The client leads, and the therapist follows" is the immutable rule of attunement. And attunement is a key component of Brainspotting, as my work with a client named Bette illustrates.

Some years ago, Bette came to me six months after she had been diagnosed as paranoid schizophrenic. She was hearing voices and felt that there was someone out to get her. Bette's symptoms began when she was in the hospital after emergency surgery to remove her ruptured spleen. Unbeknownst to her doctors, the threatening voices she heard were triggered as a side effect from the painkillers she was given. Somehow, as the symptoms worsened, her dosage of the medicine was increased. To make things worse, Bette was placed in restraints, as the medical staff feared she would harm herself. Then, when she healed from her surgery, she was placed in an inpatient psychiatric facility. Bette was prescribed heavy doses of antipsychotics, which sedated her at best.

As the side effects from the painkillers wore off, she gradually got her feet back on the ground. Bette was released from the psychiatric facility with a prescription for the antipsychotics, which she promptly threw away. But she knew something was wrong because she still heard the voices rumbling in her head. While researching the side effects of antipsychotics, Bette discovered that for a small percentage of the population, painkillers can cause paranoia and hallucinations as a side effect.

"That's me!" she thought, "But why am I still hearing those voices?"

Bette received a referral to a therapist and went to the first session expecting to receive the help she needed. The therapist finished the first evaluation session and recommended she see a psychiatrist and be put back on antipsychotic meds. After all, she was still hearing voices. She refused, and the therapist would not continue to see her, labeling Bette as "treatment resistant." It took Bette six months to summon the courage to seek help again. She was referred to me by a friend whom she trusted.

In our first session, Bette reluctantly told me her story. She feared that I would think she was "crazy" and ship her out for meds, or even worse, back to the hospital. Although the voices were still present, Bette struck me as quite lucid in every other way. She wasn't trying to convince me of her sanity, in the way that clients with paranoid schizophrenia often do. Bette was simply afraid I wouldn't believe her.

I like to say, "A good therapist is a good detective." So I listened carefully for clues. The books told me one thing, but my instincts told me another. My sense was that Bette had been deeply traumatized by the surgery, the voices that emerged afterward, and the restraints. I offered to do use the Resource Model of Brainspotting with her. When I explained in detail how it worked, Bette was surprisingly receptive to the idea, considering what she had been through.

We started by having her go back to all the sights and sounds of her emergency hospitalization for her ruptured spleen. Her SUDS immediately skyrocketed to a ten, and she reported that her chest was pounding. I noticed her hands were gripping the arms of her chair, and I asked how that felt. She answered, "It's the only thing that's keeping me in this room!" We used her hands as her Body Resource. Her eyes were locked on mine, and I asked how that felt. "Somehow reassuring," she replied. So eye contact with me was her Resource Spot.

The processing sequentially followed the events of her pre- and post-surgery experience. Bette recalled that the voices started immediately as she woke up from the anesthesia. At that moment in her processing, she remembered the voices more than she actually heard them. I wondered if perhaps she had heard the voices of her doctors while under the anesthesia, but guided myself to not jump to any conclusions. Bette literally felt the restraints on her arms and legs as she remembered being tied down by the hospital aides. Her memories proceeded ahead to the psych hospitalization. She remembered the terror of being locked in a ward with acutely psychotic patients. Throughout her processing, Bette's eyes stay locked on mine, perhaps searching to see if I believed her. She even processed the negative experience of the therapist who refused to treat her when she wouldn't see a psychiatrist for medication. By the end of the session, her SUDS level was down to a two, and she felt great relief throughout her body, although she was exhausted. We arranged to meet the following week.

When Bette returned, she told me that her anxiety level had steadily climbed through the week. She was now hearing just one voice, and it was that of a male. The sensation of the restraints on her arms had also returned, and it was powerful and frightening. Her SUDS was back up to a ten. I wondered whether our last session was not as successful as I thought it had been. Again, I guided myself not to form any assumptions, but to trust Bette's process and follow it wherever it went.

Instead of bringing her back to the surgery and hospitalization, my gut told me to go right from where she was. I encouraged her to bring her awareness to the voice and the restricted feeling on her arms. Bette's eyes immediately darted to her left, toward the window in my office. Her eyes opened wide, and she screamed, "No, no, no!" Bette saw a door open, and her uncle walked in. She was back to being five years old. Bette sat transfixed as she felt him approach and take her arms and hold her down. "It's his voice!" she cried. She then remembered how he molested her daily for a year while her mother was out at work.

I immediately stepped in and guided Bette's attention back to the feeling of her hands on the arms of the chair and her feet on the ground. I encouraged her to hear the sound of my voice, to make sure she stayed as much in the present as possible. By the end of the session, she was confused and overwhelmed, but she was relieved to connect the voice with her uncle, whom she knew had been inappropriate with both her and her sister. There has been controversy in the psychology field about recovered abuse memories, and I always leave it to the client to decide on whether their memories are accurate. Either way, these images and other sensory experiences that seem to come out of nowhere can be processed with Brainspotting.

Bette continued Brainspotting sessions with me for six months, and we processed her memories of her uncle and other traumas from her childhood. It appears that the surgery, and the side effects of the painkillers, unearthed abuse memories that had been deeply buried by dissociation. None of the professionals she'd seen had picked that up. Hearing voices set off a secondary trauma spiral, in which she was incorrectly diagnosed as paranoid schizophrenic, restrained, heavily sedated, and hospitalized in a psychiatric facility. But all of these experiences were ultimately treatable with the Resource Model of Brainspotting. Bette stopped hearing voices and felt confident and strong in her body.

The work with her was extremely gratifying and yet humbling to me. I'm not immune from making mistakes. But I had entered into the process with her with no assumptions, and I didn't get side-tracked by symptoms that clearly suggested diagnoses that were not accurate. Bette led, and I followed. She was the head of the comet, and I had to work hard to get in and stay in the tail.

The core of the work with Bette was my ability to listen to her and engage her in a trusting relationship. What emerged from her history, as well as the traumas in the hospital, challenged her capacity to trust, so I had to earn it. The trauma was deep in Bette's brain and felt in her body, so in addition to the relationship, she needed the brain-body focus of the Brainspotting eye positions and processing. Years later, I came to call Brainspotting's combination of body-brain focus and therapist-client relationship the Dual Attunement Frame.

• • •

Brainspotting has had many incarnations since its beginning. In the first few years after its discovery, the attention and emphasis was more on technical developments than clinical ones. Brainspotting was so new, and there was so much to observe and absorb. From the onset, there were other therapists involved in Brainspotting. My friends and colleagues formed a nascent Brainspotting community, a source of both feedback and inquiry for me. Experimentation with eye positions and their responses ruled the day. More techniques were explored and discarded than were embraced. It was fascinating to watch, as the dynamic of exploration was open and fluid. I was trying to figure out what I had discovered and what it was, as well as what it wasn't—a process that still continues. I gave such rapt attention to the location of the Brainspots and the processing that ensued that my awareness was drawn away from the core of healing: the relationship between the therapist and client. It took me a while to develop the idea of dual attunement and even longer to wrap the concept of the frame around it.

In 2007, a few years after my initial discovery, I was preparing to present at an annual retreat. I was writing on a flipchart, trying to organize my presentation. The ideas and words started flowing, and I tried to capture them on paper as rapidly as I could. I had realized that my emphasis on the eye-position work and its processing had distracted me from my therapeutic roots, and my brain began to synthesize the technical and relational aspects of my discovery faster than I could write. In my head, I saw a double helix, intertwining the clinical and the technical. The words "clinical Brainspotting" flashed through my mind, and I wrote them at the top of the paper. I then filled every corner of the flipchart page in a scant fifteen minutes. After I'd deciphered my scrawl, I realized I had developed the entire presentation. A new line came to me: "The relationship is not meant to serve the Brainspotting; the Brainspotting is meant to serve the relationship." Since then, I have spoken those words countless times at trainings and speeches. It is a point worth repeating—in fact, it is a point vital to understanding Brainspotting.

Fast forward to October 2009. I had developed the clinical (or relational) Brainspotting model and integrated it into the trainings. I was presenting a Brainspotting training in Boulder, Colorado, which is one of the great Brainspotting centers of the world. Enter Robert Scaer, MD, author of *The Body Bears the Burden* and *The Trauma Spectrum.* Bob is a world-class expert on the brain and psychological trauma. He has discovered that many physical conditions, such as whiplash, are dramatically exacerbated by a history of PTSD, especially PTSD derived from childhood trauma. I use Bob as a resource when neuro questions come up, which shields me from revealing any gaps in my knowledge on the subject. At this Boulder training, Bob, in answering a question, waxed eloquent on the "exquisite attunement" of Brainspotting and the way it follows the client both relationally and neurologically. I felt like a lightning bolt had struck me. In a few sentences, Bob had captured the core of Brainspotting: it was the therapist's attunement not only to the client as a person, but also to the brain of the client that explained why Brainspotting is so powerful and unique. Immediately I paid attention to how this simultaneous attunement occurred in my work with my clients.

I knew I had to come up with a name worthy of the phenomenon. While studying the mechanisms of EMDR, I learned the concept of dual attention. Basically, when a person is attending to two different things at the same time, the brain is more open to change. It seems that dual attention makes the brain more receptive to traveling down new neural pathways when confronting the same experiences. It stands to reason that Brainspotting uses dual attention (perhaps even triple attention); clients focus on an eye position with body awareness while tracking their internal process. So my mind played with the sound and rhythm of *dual attention* and came up with the term *dual attunement.*

This term captures the essence of the endeavor of Brainspotting. The therapist has to multitask in order to closely follow the different levels of client communication, while at the same time following the client's eye/brain/body cues. Paying attention to all these elements is a highly challenging balancing act, not for the faint of heart or the weak of will. It is never an easy task for even me, the developer of Brainspotting.

• • •

The neural attunement aspect of Brainspotting has taught me much about the person-to-person attunement of the listening process. The way I listen now to my clients is starkly different from how I listened before Brainspotting. I am thinking of their brain all the time, and I'm seeing and feeling information flowing down the vast, complex synaptic highways as I listen to their story. And it has shown me that what I thought the client was communicating is often quite different than I had believed.

Communication is all about encoding and decoding. The speaker encodes their message, and the listener decodes it. But I have observed that much more is lost in this translation than we ever realize. We often believe we are understanding the encoded message when we are not, just as we believe our encodings are being effectively decoded when they are not. In the therapy office, the healing process can rise or fall based on the relative success of this encode-decode communication process. Relational therapists live and die by how well they listen. Good listening on the part of the analyst is the core of Freud's "talking cure," as well as most interpersonal therapies. After all, how good can any technique be if the therapists can't listen well to their clients? I was taught this listening model in my analytic training, and it has served me well my entire career. Enhancing my listening skills has been an ongoing developmental process for me in my decades as a therapist.

But Brainspotting and my studies of the brain have drastically altered how I listen. When I learned that there are up to one quadrillion connections in the brain, I knew I couldn't have a clue as to what was going on inside it. That realization was actually liberating for me. Since we can't know the unknowable, how is it that therapists can know anything? The answer is, by listening carefully and intently to what the client tells us, and by not assuming we can know anything else. We receive exactly what they say, in the order they say it. That's it—anything else is an assumption, an imposition of the processes of our own brain.

This kind of listening demands a great deal of focus. It requires therapists to notice and brush aside their own thoughts, including the wise, informed, intuitive observations that come to their minds. This kind of listening takes practice and demands that the therapist constantly seek a blank, Zen state. At best, we find and lose this state repeatedly. I still work at it every day and know I will always have to.

As we clear away our inner process, we can then begin to carefully attend to the client's communications, word for word, sentence by sentence. Every human speaks a different language. The same words and phrases in the same language mean different things to different people. Sometimes the variation is nuanced; at other times, it is drastic. So it is incumbent on us to learn and use the client's language. It is crucial to not change a word or phrase when we communicate back to a client, as altering words risks changing their meaning. Carefully using the client's precise wording provides both attunement and mirroring to them. This reflective listening can help heal both the soul and the brain, if provided consistently and for long enough.

Even when the therapist is silent, the client is always aware of the Brainspotting therapist's witnessing presence. I know this because my clients tell me so when I ask. Dual attunement means that relational presence is integrated with the technical, brain-based aspect of Brainspotting.

• • •

In my early training, I was taught that there is the presenting problem and then there is the real problem. I have found this to be untrue. The presenting problem *is* the real problem. It neurobiologically and existentially embodies the client's conscious and unconscious struggle. It may be emotional, cognitive, behavioral, or relational. When the presenting problem is resolved, the treatment is completed.

I am not a behaviorist, mind you. I simply believe that the client always knows best. The problem is in their brain and the solution is in their brain. Just as the customer is always right, so is the client. Certainly clients need psycho-education (a term that amuses me) to understand the Brainspotting process and to effectively co-participate in it. I also provide my clients a clear, basic education of how their brain works, and I refer back to this information often throughout the treatment. I am amazed by how clients respond to this brain information with, "That makes sense" and "I find that relieving." My observation is that the conscious, thinking brain can easily go astray, but the intuitive brain does not. We know what we know, and deep inside is where we know it. When a therapist affirms this inner wisdom by listening carefully and trusting what the client has to say, the client feels attuned to as they may never have before. This is deeply healing unto itself.

So isn't attunement an issue for all therapy and not just Brainspotting? Well, yes and no. Yes, because these principles of attunement apply to all therapy approaches that are based on the relationship between the client and the therapist. No, because there are limits to how much a therapist can reach a client with verbal interchange alone. Talking reaches only the areas of the brain that possess language. This leaves out the right, mid-, and hindbrains, where our intuitive, emotional, and body awareness reside.

Brainspotting plumbs the visual field for spots that hold and reveal resonance in our deeper brain. Outside Window Brainspotting finds them by means of the therapist observing the client's reflexive responses. Inside Window Brainspotting finds them by means of the therapist helping the client identify the eye position where a client feels the most activation, somatically or experientially. And with Gazespotting, the client spontaneously, without direction from the therapist, looks to these points of access in their visual field. By guiding clients to and/or noticing these Brainspots with the client, therapists interact with clients in a different and deeper way than they do in the most attuned of talk therapies.

But the Brainspotting process doesn't end there—it begins there. The client is already activated around the issue on which they want to work. They are aware of where they are holding the activation in their body. Together, the Brainspotting therapist and the client are looking at a spot that correlates to their inner brain-body experience. Then the client mindfully observes their inner process, wherever it goes, while periodically reporting on it to the therapist, who listens to these communications with openness and curiosity. The therapist, without assumption, follows the client's process, wherever it goes, and waits for the surprises the client could never anticipate or even dream of. Therefore, the therapist is both witness to and participant in the client's healing process. What occurs would never happen if the therapist and client were simply conversing. Yet, they *are* conversing, but only in the context of the client's processing on the Brainspot. This healing phenomenon is unique, and in my experience, could not be evinced in any other manner. It represents the quintessence of the Dual Attunement Frame. It is this simultaneity of the relational and neurobiological attunement that synergistically fosters focused, powerful, deep processing that leads to healing resolution.

The therapist's role in the Brainspotting process, regardless of which model of Brainspotting is being used, is to provide an attuned, mirroring container for the client. To do so, the therapist creates a *frame* that holds and defines the client within their own inner experience.

• • •

The brain is a problem-solving mechanism that simultaneously processes the internal and external landscape. The brain's most important function is to promote physical survival. With that accomplished, the brain attempts to help a person continually adapt to attain and maintain homeostasis. When a person comes to a Brainspotting therapist, it means they have identified problems that they haven't been able to solve on their own. Their infinite neural system has not been able to either identify the problem or correct it.

All parts of the brain are communicating with each other all the time. This communication includes direct messaging between the most primitive area (the brainstem) and the most advanced area (the neocortex) of the brain. To me, a breakdown in the brain's capacity to effectively process anything is essentially a breakdown in communication. Somehow the message is not getting out, in, or through. In my opinion, this communication breakdown is the cause of all problems that individuals bring to therapists. This is particularly true in the case of trauma. Because trauma overwhelms the brain's capacity to fully process the incident, one can readily see how traumatic experiences would not be responsive to talk therapy alone, with its limited brain-body reach.

However, not only is the problem in the client's brain and neural system, but the solution is as well. The Dual Attunement Frame of Brainspotting helps the client's brain and body heal itself from the inside out. The ideal frame leads to the ideal processing, which results in the optimal resolution. But the wisdom is not in the therapist; it is in the genius of the client's nervous system.

In Brainspotting, the therapist creates the neurobiological frame by finding the resonant eye positions with the client, who is activated around their issue of choice. The therapist then guides the client to maintain their focus on the spot and mindfully observe their inner process, step by step. The therapist then tracks the client's processing closely, yet openly, wherever it goes. This attuned, witnessing presence provides the relational frame known in other therapies as the *holding environment.* In Brainspotting, this relational frame is continually focused by the therapist and client attending to the Brainspot, the body sensations, and the processing.

This frame exists within the continuum from the most activating to the most resourced of all forms of Brainspotting. The Activation Model not only finds the Brainspot of greatest activation, but it also gives the most relational latitude and space to the client. Although very present, the therapist may be relatively inactive if the processing is proceeding effectively. And yet the client always feels the therapist's presence. I frequently ask my clients how much they felt me there and how helpful my presence was. Their response is usually some version of "I couldn't do it without you."

In the Resource Model, the Brainspot is determined by the Body Resource (the place of calm or groundedness in the body) and the Resource Spot that matches it. But clients using the Resource Model usually need the therapist to be more interactive. Many such clients had insufficient bonding with early caretakers, and as a result, have what therapists call attachment issues. These individuals easily feel lost and anxious if the therapist is not active enough. Accordingly, the therapist checks in more frequently with these vulnerable clients during the course of a session. Some clients even need a running dialogue to maintain their groundedness. But this doesn't mean there is something wrong with these clients. It's simply what their brain-body systems, compromised by neglect or abuse, need. In Brainspotting, as therapists, we say that we are using a "tighter frame" in these cases.

Setting the space within the frame is part of the attunement process. It is not unusual for Brainspotting therapists to adjust the frame on the fly, sometimes stepping in more, sometimes stepping back quickly. The Activation Model can be shifted toward greater use of the Resource Model when necessary. And when a vulnerable client heals, they can be shifted gradually toward a greater use of the Activation Model. Following the client's process and needs in the moment is all a matter of attunement.

The tail does not lead the head of the comet. The head always leads the tail. The Dual Attunement Frame is how the Brainspotting therapist works to get into the tail and hang in there, as much as humanly possible.

CHAPTER 7

Brainspotting as an Integrative Model

There Is No Turf When It Comes to Healing

Sigmund Freud is regarded by many, including me, as the father of modern psychology. He attracted an inner circle of devotees that regularly studied together with him. In time, many of Freud's disciples challenged his notions and broke away from him, forming their own schools of thought—C. G. Jung, Alfred Adler, and Otto Rank, for example. These defections led to a splintering of Freud's core theories and practices. In the decades that followed the breaking apart of Freud's inner circle, hundreds of other therapy methods have emerged, including both cognitive and behavioral approaches, which espouse ideas quite opposite to Freud's. (Interestingly, common ground between the cognitive and behavioral approaches led to their integration into what is called cognitive behavioral therapy, or CBT. But as time has passed, splits have re-emerged in the CBT community.)

During my decades in the psychotherapy field, I have been exposed to many highly effective approaches, such as gestalt, hypnosis, psychodrama, body-oriented, and existential therapies. Undoubtedly,

I am leaving out many more of my direct and indirect influences than I have included on this list. Perhaps the existence of so many effective therapy approaches is a true reflection of the complexity of the human system. And with advances in brain science, we are still learning more about this intricate system every day.

Therapists used to be purists much more than they tend to be now. The term *eclectic* used to almost be almost a put-down when applied to therapists. It reflected that a therapist was not only not committed to any therapy approach, but also that they were not firmly grounded in any method. Today, the term *eclectic* generally means that the therapist uses whatever works with a given client. It suggests that the techniques a therapist uses are highly individualized and not generalizable from client to client.

The term *integrative* is much more in vogue at present. There are even schools of thought that are actually called *integrative psychotherapy.* Many, if not most, therapists recognize the need to be integrative in their practices today. Therapists commonly study more than one method in order to face the daily challenges in their offices. It's not clear if clients are bringing more complex issues to therapy now or if advances in the field help therapists to identify clients' complexities better. It takes many years of experience to become a good therapist. This wisdom entails learning what to say and when and how to say it. But it also includes knowing what not to say. Experience leading to wisdom gives therapists the ability to integrate different techniques into their overall approach.

I was originally trained as a psychoanalyst and psychodynamic psychotherapist. I took many trainings and seminars over my decades of practice, and became more active and interactive with my clients than I was originally taught to do. But the acute listening I learned in my analytic roots always stayed with me.

My prior training and experience was challenged when I studied EMDR, as it was such a new paradigm. It went against my nature to become a purist with EMDR. I wanted to learn this new method to the highest of levels of proficiency; however, I couldn't keep myself from experimenting with EMDR. The method carried a powerful set of tools that begged to be explored. I innovated with BioLateral Sound and continuous (uninterrupted) stimulation, and I integrated EMDR with the psychodynamic approach. To me, the processing that happened with EMDR was another version of the free association that was pivotal to the analysis approach I'd learned so many years earlier. With my exposure to and study of somatic experiencing, there was even more for me to integrate. Just the deep observation of the body experience was rich, new territory for me, but the idea of using the resources that the body holds was particularly game-changing. I pulled all of this knowledge and experience together into Natural Flow EMDR, my own integrative culmination at that moment. So I was primed to integrate when I discovered Brainspotting.

I have made integration with other approaches a cornerstone of the Brainspotting method. Brainspotting is designed as an open, intuitive, breathing model that reflects how open and intuitive the human system is. The Dual Attunement Frame of Brainspotting, discussed in the last chapter, is an essential integration of brain-based attunement and attunement to the therapeutic relationship. Daniel Siegel, MD, in his own independent studies, has named this combination *interpersonal neurobiology.*

When therapists come to Brainspotting Phase 1 trainings, they are encouraged, by the trainer, to not leave their other approaches at the door. Many trainees are surprised to hear that it is not only OK to integrate Brainspotting into their current methods, but that therapists are expected to do so. Keep in mind that therapists don't come to study new techniques because they aren't successful with what they are already doing. Good therapists are aware that they need to continually pursue new learning. There is an old saying, "The more you know, the more you know what you don't know." Therapists never stop learning, even if they practice well into their eighties. How can it be that one method covers all the bases for the human system, when that system is essentially infinite in its complexity?

I have a saying, "There is no turf when it comes to healing." Many other approaches have fallen into the trap of becoming hierarchical or demanding purity in the application of their techniques. In research, fidelity is required, but if it is too closely adhered to in clinical work, it can derail the attunement. If therapists are paying too much attention to getting a method's protocols and procedures right, how can they closely follow the client's process? Psychotherapy is both an art and a science, and in Brainspotting I embrace and teach this dualism. Brainspotting trainees frequently say to me, "Thank you for giving me permission to be flexible." I often answer, "Why would you let anyone else take that permission away from you?" The general public usually assigns authority to therapists who are perceived as being wise and knowledgeable. Yet therapists are frequently more vulnerable than most people realize. Each person is a unique individual, and that includes the therapist. Thus, each therapy process—in fact, each session—is different. What remains the same is the client's need to be listened to very carefully.

• • •

There are many ways that Brainspotting can be integrated with other approaches. As I described in the last chapter, the Dual Attunement Frame is the fundamental integration of the relational and neurobiological attunement. If the therapist and the client are both lucky, the processing in this Dual Attunement Frame will be pure and will resolve the problem at hand. In practice, that rarely happens, because humans are so complex and unpredictable. By the time someone has made it to a therapist's office, they have usually been struggling for many months, if not years. Most problems are complicated and have their origins in childhood. Trauma and retraumatizations are often part of the client's picture. Complex issues are not held in one part of the brain; they infiltrate the entire brain.

The complexity of clients' issues and brains leads Brainspotting therapists to rely on their other methods when it comes to both understanding and intervening with clients during sessions. But these other methods are used while the client remains focused on the Brainspot. The eye position, or Brainspot, provides definition and containment no matter what other techniques are brought into the process.

Brainspotting trainees come from all backgrounds and every orientation. Many Brainspotting students are already trained in EMDR, somatic experiencing, and hypnosis. But just as many trainees come from methods as diverse as family therapy, Jungian analysis, bioenergetics, neuro-linguistic programming, and cognitive behavioral therapy. Each type of therapist intervenes differently on a Brainspot when needed. An analytically trained Brainspotting therapist might make a transference or resistance interpretation. A Brainspotting hypnotherapist might use suggestion. A CBT-trained Brainspotting therapist might employ cognitive restructuring. A breathwork Brainspotting therapist might guide the client through some breathing exercises. But all these interventions are more effective because they are framed and focused by attending to the Brainspot. If all these different therapists were well trained and attuned to the client, their interventions will likely be effective. And if somehow they were less than successful, the therapists would know to step back to wait and see what happens next.

Good therapists know that all therapy work is trial and error. They don't do something because they know what's going to happen. They do something because they think it might help, and then they sit back and see what happens. Good therapists are as ready to be wrong as they are to be right. This is all part of the therapy process. Clients are usually forgiving when a therapist is off-base, as long as the therapist listens to and trusts the client. A therapist learning from a mistake made in therapy can be a corrective experience for the client, who can observe the therapist as both fallible and willing to admit and correct their own errors.

When therapists step in with other techniques while doing Brainspotting, the hope is that the intervention will work, and the therapist will then be able to step back. Some therapists get reinforced by the success of an integrative technique, so they continue to use it repeatedly. They don't recognize that when a client is well framed on a Brainspot, most of what goes on is self-corrective healing. A good intervention unblocks an impeded process, which allows the process to resume flowing on its own. The brain knows what to do—and 99 percent of the time, it knows what to do better than the therapist does. The Brainspotting therapist's job is to know what to do during that 1 percent of the time they are called upon to step in.

• • •

The following story exemplifies how integrating another approach with Brainspotting can be essential in reaching a healing resolution. Wes came to me with a driving phobia that started a year earlier, after he had been in two car accidents in one month. The second crash was more serious than the first, as he was broadsided by a car that ran a red light. Although Wes wasn't seriously injured, his car was totaled. He then rented a replacement vehicle, and every time he drove it, he became increasingly anxious. Wes avoided the intersection where he was hit. (Avoidance is a classic PTSD symptom.) Gradually his anxiety increased, and he drove less and less. He stopped driving on highways and then had his wife drive whenever they were together in the car. Finally, Wes stopped driving altogether.

We began his therapy with some pretty standard Inside Window Brainspotting. We started by processing the first and lesser accident. In ten minutes, it was released from start to finish. Single-event traumas in adulthood often process through quickly because they appear to be more contained in one area of the brain. Childhood and repeated traumas tend to infiltrate more of the brain and therefore are more difficult to resolve.

The second accident was much more challenging. I guided Wes to bring up the first moment he knew he was going to be broadsided. He saw the car to his right, in his peripheral vision. His SUDS level shot up to a nine, and he felt the jolt of the impact. Traumatic events tend to be recorded sequentially in the brain. In Brainspotting, they also tend to process through sequentially, step by step. That's why Brainspotting therapists are taught to start by asking clients to recall the first moment they knew that something bad was about to happen.

Wes's experience processing through the second accident was dramatically different than his processing of the first one. This time around, the processing was slow and arduous, with high levels of activation. In his body, Wes not only relived the impact on his head and neck, but he also felt a deep anxiety in his chest. Even the Resource Model, with the calming and grounding afforded by the Body Resource and Resource Spot, was limited in its effectiveness.

I decided to integrate Brainspotting with a technique from hypnosis called an affect bridge. I guided Wes to ask himself for an earlier life issue that might somehow be associated with this accident. While he was still gazing intently at the pointer, a memory popped up in his mind. Wes's eyes widened as his tears welled up. When he was five years old, he and his family were in a car accident on the way to church. His father was driving, and Wes and his sister were in the back of the car. Mother was in the front, in the passenger seat, and Wes was seated directly behind her. Guess what? Their car was broadsided from the right! The car was totaled, and both Wes and his mother were injured and hospitalized. Fortunately both recovered, but his mother was in the hospital for a month with a fractured vertebrae.

This childhood memory processed through surprising quickly. And after it resolved, the second accident, from a year earlier, released more easily than before as well.

I then guided Wes through some focused Brainspotting work on his remaining, but now reduced, driving phobia. That fear processed down to a zero SUDS as well. But that is not the end of the story.

Week after week, Wes would come into our session and not tell me whether he had resumed driving. When I asked, he was evasive, but admitted he hadn't tried yet. The accidents had been processed through and his driving phobia was contained, so what was the problem? The remaining anticipatory anxiety about driving was still blocking him. In the face of all his healing, this block might seem odd, but I had encountered it before. Anticipatory anxiety can take on a life of its own. This state of mind can hang on after everything else has been resolved. Anticipatory anxiety can even block the power of Brainspotting.

I knew it was time to integrate in some exposure therapy. I asked Wes, "How did you come to the session today?"

"My wife drove me" was his answer.

"Is she still here with the car?"

"She's in the waiting room." Wes knew where I was heading with this line of inquiry.

I said, "I'll drive you to a secluded street a few blocks from here. Then you can get behind the wheel with me in the passenger seat."

Wes agreed, and off we went. I drove, and when we arrived at the designated location, we switched seats. Wes was shocked that he was calm. With the anticipation behind him, so was the anxiety. Wes started up the car and drove without a problem. He looked over at me and said, "Can I drive you back to the office?" Who was I to object?

When we returned to the office, we located the Brainspot that correlated with his successful performance. He now felt pride in his chest instead of anxiety. Wes drove his wife home from the office, with his driving phobia and avoidance behind him, in the rearview mirror.

It was clear to me that despite Wes's remarkable emotional healing from his car accidents, including the one from childhood, Brainspotting alone would not have resolved his driving phobia. *In vivo,* or real-life, exposure was necessary. Wes, like all humans, was complex. And complex problems sometimes require the creative, informed, intuitive integration of therapeutic approaches, even when using the highly effective Brainspotting.

CHAPTER 8

Z-Axis and Convergence Brainspotting

Brainspotting in Three Dimensions

Ellen was stuck in a destructive relationship with her boss. Well, Paul wasn't exactly her boss. He was supposed to be Ellen's partner in a lucrative party-supply business they had started eight years earlier. But as the years passed and the business grew, Paul had gradually taken over. They had both worked equally hard, but Ellen hadn't asserted herself when Paul had put the business in his name. "Don't worry, I'll take care of you. We're partners," Paul had reassured her. Every time Ellen had asked for just compensation, Paul had put her off with, "All of the profits are going back into the business." She was easily manipulated and unable to assert herself. Ellen revealed to me that, on some level, she didn't feel she deserved her share. This feeling traced back to an abusive family pattern where her older brother was the favored one. Ellen told me, "I was the Cinderella. When I asked for something, my parents told me I was selfish and greedy. Eventually I started believing it."

Distorted beliefs are deep-seated and can be hard to change. Even with Brainspotting, it can take time to find the source of these beliefs and release them. No matter what type of Brainspotting I used with Ellen, nothing seemed to make a difference. We tried every combination of Inside and Outside Window, Gazespotting, and One-Eye Brainspotting. Even the Resource Model could not budge her. So I experimented with something I had just learned; it was called visual convergence therapy.

Her activation spot was to her right and above eye level. For this new approach, it was necessary that Ellen be able to look at the eye position up close. I handed her the pointer and had her line up the tip of it with her Brainspot, about a foot away from her face. I then guided Ellen to look through the tip of the pointer to the most distant spot in the room. She found it on the wall, directly behind and beyond the pointer tip. I instructed her to go back and forth between looking at the pointer and looking at the spot on the wall every five seconds, for a full minute.

After trying out this technique, Ellen reported, "That was strange. I felt all the anxiety drain out of me as I was going back and forth. My chest feels much better now." I instructed Ellen to continue the procedure. She accomplished more in the next twenty minutes of processing, with the convergence, than she had in the prior three months of Brainspotting therapy. In two sessions of this new back-and-forth, close-and-far work, Ellen was able to deeply heal and release her distorted beliefs of unworthiness. She was also able to confront Paul and not be sidetracked by his manipulations or counter-aggression.

I was blown away by Ellen's response to doing convergence on the Brainspot. I have since observed that about 5 to 10 percent of my clients, who respond to nothing else, do well with this back-and-forth approach. For these individuals, as it was for Ellen, it has been a godsend. It has been a blessing for me as well. Once again, using the experimental, integrative model, I discovered how to use visual convergence therapy with Brainspotting through trial and error.

• • •

Here is the story of how I found out about visual convergence therapy.

I was giving a Brainspotting training in 2006 in Pittsburgh. On the final day, one of the trainees handed me a paper, saying, "Read this. I think you'll find it interesting with what you are doing." The paper was titled "Visual Convergence Therapy as a Vagal Maneuver: An Unexpected Palliative for Anginal Pain and Related Issues." It was authored by Merrill Bowan, a neuro-optometrist, and it was actually his draft of an article that had never been published.

The paper contained a host of terms that were foreign to me, like *extraocular muscles, oculocardiac reflex,* and *visual convergence therapy.* The extraocular muscles (EOMs) are the six muscles that hold each eyeball in place. Because humans are binocular, or see with two eyes, these muscles have to constantly work together, adjusting both eyes independently, to maintain our focused vision. This is a crucial, complex, delicate task. Not only our capacity to see clearly, but also our capability to survive, depends on these twelve muscles attached to our eyeballs. Accordingly, the EOMs contain many nerve endings and are the source of the oculocardiac reflex (OCR). The OCR is a primitive, yet powerful, immediate parasympathetic, or body-calming, reflex. The OCR can be activated either by pressing on the eyeballs or by quickly converging (moving together) then diverging (moving apart) the eyes. When we look at a close object, our eyes converge, and when we look in the distance, our eyes diverge. Accordingly, when we intentionally look back and forth, or from close to far, we can deliberately activate the OCR. Repeatedly looking back and forth, close and far, is what I used to great effect with Ellen on her Brainspot.

Let me bring you back to the challenging title of Bowan's article and explain it a bit further. He calls the therapy of activating the OCR a "vagal maneuver." That means the OCR affects the vagus nerve, which runs from the brain directly down to the heart and the stomach. The activated vagus nerve sends an immediate signal to slow the heart and relax the body. According to Bowan, this slowdown in heart rate helps to reduce not only angina pains in the heart, but to ease intense feelings of anxiety as well.

Bowan, an innovator in his field of optometry, gave a case example in his paper. He helped a patient significantly reduce her panic attacks by using visual convergence therapy (also called simply convergence therapy, or CT). He had his patient hold her finger twelve inches from her eyes and move her gaze back and forth, between her close finger and the far wall, every two seconds, for a period of two minutes. Bowan reported that his patient remained panic free for a year after a series of CT treatments.

The fact that a nontherapist could effectively treat an emotional condition supports my belief that the answers to our psychological issues lie deep in our brains and bodies. Bowan treated a panic disorder by activating the OCR, a primitive reflex that accesses the vagus nerve, slowing the heart and calming the body. There was no talking, no analyzing, and no cognitive interventions—just results.

• • •

With Ellen, I superimposed the convergence therapy on her activated eye position. Keep in mind that there was nothing truly psychological about her Brainspot. It was just the location in visual space where Ellen felt her body tighten when she thought about Paul's behavior toward her. By putting Brainspotting together with the visual convergence therapy, I was using one reflex (the OCR) to calm down (or discharge) another reflex (the tightening in Ellen's chest). This was simply a body-to-body process. As Ellen was able to release the reaction she was stuck with regarding Paul, her distorted beliefs of unworthiness also vanished. I wondered if I could have a similar effect with other stuck clients.

I began experimenting with a new model I called Convergence Brainspotting, using it with any of my clients that I thought might benefit from it. For some, it made a big difference in accelerating their process and bringing them change and relief. For others, it seemed to make little difference, so I had to keep experimenting with new techniques and combinations of techniques with them.

• • •

Visual convergence therapy also brought to my attention something obvious that I had missed: the visual field is three-dimensional. Up to the moment I used the convergence therapy with Ellen, I had been limited to using the x and y axes on a flat, two-dimensional plane. Inside Window Brainspotting started with the x axis of left and right. It was then expanded two-dimensionally to the y axis of up or down, at the suggestion of my clients. Convergence work got me thinking three-dimensionally. This new close-and-far work opened up the entire visual field to my exploration. Martha Jacobi, a colleague of mine from New York and math major in college, suggested the term *z axis* for the dimension of depth.

Meanwhile, another colleague in Colorado, Roger Reynolds, was also reporting exciting results using Brainspotting with depth, as he moved the pointer close and far to help release whiplash symptoms from car-crash survivors. I started to reflect on whether I could expand my use of convergence by slowing down the back-and-forth movements along the z axis. I also wondered if different distances on a Brainspot, closer or further away, might carry more or less charge for clients.

So once again, I began experimenting. I was startled by what I found. There was almost always a difference between looking close or looking far on a Brainspot. For most clients, the difference was striking. Looking farther away on the spot usually lowered the SUDS level. However, with 10 to 25 percent of clients, looking close on the Brainspot made them feel calmer and looking farther away was more activating.

It made sense that focusing on an object or spot farther away would make a person feel calmer and the spot less dangerous. In the animal kingdom, a predator feels more threatening the closer it is and, by contrast, less threatening if it is farther away. Have you ever watched a television nature show where zebras were grazing, with lions in their view, a few hundred feet away? It can strike us as odd that the zebras wouldn't bolt at the sight and the smell of their predators. We feel like calling to the zebras, saying, "Run, run, run for your life!" We are clearly identifying with the zebras and also revealing our shared animal heritage of the fight-flight reflex. The zebras know they are out of striking distance from the lions, but they vigilantly are keeping a close watch. When the lions stealthily close the gap and get too close, the zebras become skittish and walk, or run if necessary, to create more distance.

As the pointer is moved closer to a client who is activated around an issue, their anxiety level tends to rise and the SUDS level goes up. The client rationally knows it is only a pointer in the hand of a therapist, and yet the threat response is activated. That response heavily suggests that instinctual forces are at play. It reinforces my belief that psychological forces are always physiologically driven. With greater proximity, we are inducing the same threat reaction in humans that arises in animals. This is the fight, flight, or freeze response that is often experienced by humans as anxiety.

So why would a small percentage of clients react to the pointer closer up as more comforting and farther away as more unsafe? It doesn't appear to make sense. I pondered that for a long time before a client gave me a clue.

Stacey's mother was sick with cancer throughout Stacey's infancy and early childhood. Her mother was hospitalized many times and died when Stacey was six. Stacey, who came to see me in her early forties, had many memories of her mother being taken away in an ambulance. She also remembered many instances of not being allowed into her mother's hospital room. Instead, she was left standing at the door, yearning to be close to her mother.

During Brainspotting sessions, Stacey felt much more comforted looking at the pointer up close. Her anxiety rose as she looked past the pointer to the wall. At times, when I asked her to go from looking close to looking far, her arm and hand rose up, reaching out instinctively. I once pointed this out to her, and she responded, "My mother feels so out of reach."

This experience has led me to speculate that people with attachment issues may feel calmer looking close and more distressed looking off at a distance. Attachment problems are found in people with early, repeated losses or instability in their relationship to their primary caretaker, usually their mother. If my hypothesis about close and far is true, it still reflects more of a physical than psychological phenomenon.

• • •

In addition to the fast back-and-forth convergence, I developed a more gradual z-axis approach. In One-Eye Brainspotting, we utilize the difference in activation levels between right and left eyes. I like to call it "splitting the difference." I realized that we could also split the difference in the levels of activation between close and far along the z axis, just as we do between left and right eyes.

I observed that some clients processed more quickly and effectively when they used far and close more specifically. We would start by using the basic steps to find an Inside Window Brainspot, although one can also use z axis with Outside Window Brainspotting. Next, I asked the client to first look at the tip of the pointer and tell me their SUDS level of activation. Then I would guide the client to look directly through the pointer to the most distant spot in the room, which was usually the wall. It could also be the floor or ceiling, if they were looking downward or upward. I would then ask for the SUDS level on the far spot. There was usually a numerical difference between close and far (like an eight close and a five far). Sometimes the difference was small, and sometimes it was significant. As I described earlier, usually close was a higher SUDS level and far was lower.

I guided clients to start by gazing at the lower SUDS distance for about ten minutes. After that, I would have them shift their gaze to the higher SUDS distance, usually the close distance. I retook the SUDS to see if it had changed from its original level. I found that consistently processing at the far spot lowered the activation level at the close spot, and the reverse was just as true. After ten minutes, I switched back to the other distance, taking the SUDS level again. I was surprised how continually shifting the distances on the z axis seemed to accelerate the processing.

In general, I have observed that any change in how and where we look brings about a change in brain state and pushes the healing process ahead. This includes periodically closing our eyes and then opening them. Along the z axis, I would guide the client to spend progressively less time on each distance, shifting back and forth more rapidly. Starting from ten minutes close and ten far, we next proceeded to about seven and seven, then to five and five, and then to three and three. Finally, the close and far were going back and forth every minute. This tended to both keep the process moving and propel it forward. The more active the brain is, the more it tends to move information around its vast circuitry, facilitating change and promoting healing.

Eventually, the z axis ends up at the original convergence pace, where the client is shifting back and forth every five seconds on the z axis, clearly activating the oculocardiac reflex. I have since found both convergence and the z axis to be invaluable tools. For some Brainspotting clients, this combination is the difference between success and failure in the process. For other clients, it moves ahead a process that was already proceeding well.

CHAPTER 9

The Neurobiology of Brainspotting

It's All Brain Stuff

My training as a therapist began in the 1970s at Yeshiva University School of Social Work and was deepened in the early 1980s at the Society for Psychoanalytic Study and Research, where I was trained as a psychoanalyst. What struck me back then was that teachers and therapists always spoke of the mind and never the brain. I often wondered, "Where is the mind?" My internal answer usually was, "It must be in the brain."

And lo and behold, the 1990s emerged as the decade of the brain. What scientists learned in the 1990s led to a revolutionary shift in how we understood the brain and how it affected everything we think, feel, and do. Unfortunately, this revolution has been slow to come to the practice of psychotherapy. Much of the mental health field still adheres to variants of talk therapy without paying attention to the neurobiological imperative driving the healing process.

In 1993, my training in EMDR opened the door to a more technical way of doing therapy, one that included eye movements, rating scales, and notably, a body orientation. When I talk about the brain in this book, I am also referring to the body, as the brain and the body are one integrated unit in the comprehensive nervous system. I don't believe in the mind-body connection because I don't believe there is any mind-body separation. As said earlier, what's in the brain is in the body, and what's in the body is in the brain.

The place of the body in mental health, recognized over a century ago by Pierre Janet and brought to prominence in the 1920s and 1930s by Wilhelm Reich, has been given its due in recent decades with therapeutic approaches such as somatic experiencing and sensorimotor psychotherapy. Yet many therapists still never ask about their client's body sensations. Additionally, trauma and dissociation, conditions highly associated with the brain and the body, are frequently ignored as contributing factors to the psychological issues that drive people to seek out therapy—despite the fact that the field of traumatology has spotlighted the role of trauma in all of our lives. When we leave the brain and body out of the therapy equation, we see only a small, fractured part of the whole picture. Treatment becomes long, unfocused, and too often, unproductive. Some clients are deemed "low-responders," and some are doomed as "nonresponders." The limitations of the treatment process are rarely seen as contributing to the less-than-desired outcome.

Brainspotting brings the brain, and thus the body, back into the therapy equation. Brainspotting accesses parts of the brain that verbal interchange can never reach, much less understand, and that is what sets it apart from more traditional talk therapy. What exactly happens in our brains during Brainspotting? Until we have definitive research, my answers are speculative.

However, *The Brain That Changes Itself*, a book by Norman Doidge, MD, details the phenomenon of neuroplasticity, the brain's ability to change throughout life by forming new neural connections. It was previously thought that by adulthood the human brain was set and unable to change. Doidge outlines many stories of how people's brains have changed in ways believed to be impossible just a few years ago. It is also now known that the brain is capable of growing new cells throughout our lifetime, a phenomenon called neurogenesis. Survivors of severe traumas have been shown to suffer shrinkage of the hippocampus—a part of the brain involved in forming, organizing, and storing information—but effective therapeutic interventions have led to hippocampal neurogenesis in trauma survivors.

I have been using Brainspotting for ten years with over one thousand clients, and have seen six thousand other Brainspotting therapists use it with equal success, accomplishing changes previously thought impossible. The results that I have observed from Brainspotting convince me that it changes the brain by affecting its neuroplasticity and perhaps also contributes to neurogenesis, the growth of new brain cells.

• • •

It is my hypothesis that the visual field is a reflection of the ongoing processes held in the brain and felt in the body. Accordingly, I believe that we can harness this visual field to gain access to neural processes and influence them. Locating Brainspots in one's visual field turns the brain's massive scanning mechanism on itself and then uses it to begin to heal the brain.

Scientists know that every human brain contains about 100 billion neurons. These brain cells are connected through 100,000 miles of axons that encompass from 100 trillion up to 1 quadrillion synaptic connections. To put these numbers in perspective, the Milky Way is made up of only 100 to 400 billion stars. These cosmic numbers testify to the vast, almost infinite, complexity of the brain.

Why are we gifted with such an impossibly powerful mechanism? My guess is so that the brain possesses the capacity to observe the body, including itself, down to a cellular and perhaps molecular level. This self-scanning process appears related to our immune system, which both identifies and solves problems in the body. In this same way, the brain both observes and corrects anomalies in the body systems. But I believe the brain also observes itself down to a neuronal and synaptic level. This Socratic "know thyself" capacity of the brain is the ultimate expression of our ability to introspect. It seems to me that our brain-body's ability to observe and heal itself is existential, as this capacity makes it possible for us to survive in and adapt to our inner and outer environments.

Let's restate these highfalutin ideas more simply. When something important bothers us, we become activated, and there are positions in our visual field that match up with the places we are holding this activation in our brain. Reflecting on where we feel the activation in our body further focuses our brain on this holding place. In previous chapters, I've shared examples of what a Brainspotting session looks like from the outside—what I ask clients to do and how they respond. With the next example, let me give you a picture of what I think is happening on the inside, in the brain, during a Brainspotting session.

Donald came to me because he was traumatized by a car accident that almost took his life. He had daily flashbacks and nightmares, and every time he drove, he was convinced another crash was coming his way. I asked him to go inside and activate himself around the accident. Donald reported seeing, hearing, and feeling the moment of impact. I then had him track the pointer I was moving across his field of vision and asked him to let me know where he felt it the most. When the pointer reached a spot on his far left, Donald pointed and said, "Right there!"

What actually happened in Donald's brain when his eyes followed my pointer to his far left and found the spot where he "felt it the most"? I think when I asked Donald to "activate himself" around the accident, his brain intuitively searched its infinite neurons and neural connections for the places the trauma of the accident was held. When he revived the accident experientially by bringing up the memory in his mind, the result was that various sites in his brain became activated. Simultaneously, the areas of Donald's brain that were not involved in the crash memory were not activated. Researchers have seen these reactions on brain scans, where parts of the brain "light up" (reflecting increased blood flow in them) as others go quiet. I believe the particular spot we found in Donald's visual field matched, or corresponded to, the spots in Donald's brain that were activated. In other words, when Donald scanned his visual field, his brain simultaneously began scanning itself for the areas of activation.

The brain solves most of its challenges on its own as a result of its gifted structure and function. What therapists call "psychological symptoms," such as anxiety attacks or flashbacks, appear when the brain is unable to sufficiently solve a problem. Either the brain can't locate the problem inside itself, or it knows where the problem is but doesn't know how to untangle it. Such unsolvable problems are often trauma based.

While Donald's gaze was on the Brainspot, I guided him to observe his inner process without judgment, step by step, wherever it traveled. Periodically, Donald reported his internal process to me, and if he didn't volunteer the information, I asked him to tell me what was happening. At times, Donald's mind replayed the car accident, and at other times, it jumped around to other life experiences, some of which seemed related to the accident and some of which did not. Donald at times saw flipping images and heard sounds, while at other times he felt mostly body sensations. At some points, his mind went blank, and at other points, he reflected on mundane daily tasks. It wasn't the content that was important—it was the process. Why? Because Donald's conscious brain was observing his unconscious brain mechanisms.

By gazing at the spot he'd found off to his far left, Donald helped his brain maintain its focus on the neural problem areas and begin to figure them out. This figuring out, or untangling, doesn't happen in a cognitive, linear fashion. It is a deep-brain process, and its complexity is way beyond the reach and comprehension of our conscious awareness. Therapists call it processing, and others would recognize this process as a form of mindfulness. As explained in detail in Chapter 2, the conscious self observes the deeper self in an open, curious, noncritical fashion. This *focused-mindfulness* processing is done in a state of what I call *focused activation* (activated with body awareness on a Brainspot), so it is more rapid, contained, and to the point than most mindfulness.

Deep-brain processes are incredibly rapid, complex, and intuitive. Because they mirror the processes the brain uses to regulate all our body functions, they are a reflection of how we literally live and breathe. If our conscious brain tries to comprehend the unconscious flow that happens when we're focused on a Brainspot, it fails. However, when our conscious brain wisely accepts its limitations and trusts our deeper brain, it is led down a path of healing and resolution. This was the ultimate outcome for Donald. He recovered from his PTSD and no longer suffered from flashbacks, nightmares, and what therapists like to call "fear of reoccurrence."

With its vast power focused, by eye position, on the areas of activation, the brain can actually watch itself neurologically solve its own psychological riddles. As I and thousands of other trained Brainspotting therapists around the world can attest, the process is amazing and at times almost miraculous.

• • •

Brainspotting also provides therapists an opportunity to educate their clients in both how the Brainspotting process works and how their brain is responding to the experience. This education makes use of the model outlined by Bonnie Badenoch in her groundbreaking book *Being a Brain-Wise Therapist: A Practical Guide to Interpersonal Neurobiology.*

While the cortical brain—the conscious, thinking brain—can be confused by the deeper brain processes it observes, it can also be educated to understand them. In fact, this observer brain is highly curious and loves to be fed information. I like to call this part of the brain the "baby genius," because like a young child, it absorbs vast amounts of information all the time, but is easily bored or distracted. When you engage this baby genius, it locks onto you and everything you say.

When explaining Brainspotting, therapists engage and educate this baby genius, and in doing so, help the conscious, cortical brain accept the deeper brain's complex, nonlinear processes. For example, here is what I say to educate the baby genius about Brainspotting:

> Where you look affects how you feel. In other words, when you look left or right or up or down, you experience things differently. The difference may be slight or very noticeable. And when you focus on something that you have strong feelings about, this looking left-right or up-down difference will be more pronounced.
>
> So why do you react differently when you look in different directions? Well, shifting your eye position somehow changes what's happening in your brain, although we are not sure yet how that works. You may think that you are aware of everything that goes on inside of you, but your brain is a vast universe. When you look at this universe, you may think you see all of it. Don't be fooled—you are only seeing a small part of it. It's like when you look at the surface of the ocean—you can think you see it all, but down below the surface, where you can't see, is where most of the vast ocean exists. Brainspotting will help you to find more about your vast, complicated brain. But you need to learn that rules that are different than you are used to apply down there.

And here's what I say to help prepare the cortical brain for what happens when the deeper brain begins untangling the problem that is the focus:

> As you look at this spot, I want you to observe wherever your mind goes. This observation is a form of mindfulness. You don't direct where your mind goes—it just happens. Where it goes may make sense to you or not, but it doesn't matter. Your deeper brain knows what to do. It's like breathing. Thoughts,

memories, feelings, or body sensations may come or go. Do not judge this; just simply follow along. Trust your instincts.

Some clients take naturally to this focused-mindfulness process, while others struggle at first. In our Western culture, we have been trained to follow the linear and mistrust the intuitive.

It is interesting that vulnerability to performance issues often shows up early in the process. Clients can misread their natural processing and feel they are not "doing it right," when they are actually "performing" exactly as they should. This vulnerability reveals a cortical brain that mistrusts the deeper brain and is in need of education about itself.

Clients at times pull back from the process, saying, "I don't like how that makes me feel." On these occasions, I bring out the brainwise guidance: "Don't react to your reactions. Observe them with curiosity and see where they go." In sessions, and in life, people inhibit themselves because they are confused by and afraid of their emotional and body experiences. Clients need to be guided to see that what their bodies and emotions are telling them is relevant and meaningful feedback. This guidance helps people not only to become more self-aware, but also to become more integrated.

The ultimate education for the client comes later on in the Brainspotting process, when I instruct them to return to their original issue and see how it resonates now. "What does it look like?" I ask. "What does it feel like? How does your body feel?" Most important in this process is the retaking of the SUDS level. Even if clients don't understand the rapid, intuitive processing, they do understand when their SUDS level has dropped significantly, such as from a nine to a three. This is where the nonlinear becomes linear. The client started with the activation level of nine, with all its components. They did the processing while focused on the Brainspot, and the SUDS is now a three. A led to B, which led to C. That's the "aha" moment when the cortical brain puts all the information together and comes to understand itself and the process better.

There is something about this shift in self-awareness that seems to enhance the continued processing as well.

• • •

Therapists are creatures of habit and seem to have a sense of what works and why it works in therapy. Yet educating clients about how their brains work does not seem that powerful, or even relevant, to many therapists. I myself have been surprised by how much of a difference acquiring brain knowledge makes to clients. Not only do clients uniformly report, "That makes sense," but they also reply, "That makes me feel better."

I frequently encourage clients to download pictures of the brain from the Internet. The written information on most brain websites is too complex for the general public; at times, it's even over my head. Ironically, the websites that describe the brain for children can be the most informative for adults.

In my office, I also have a model of the brain that I use to explain and demonstrate directly how the brain gets traumatized and how it can heal. It is not unusual for me to have a person touch the back of their head and neck to feel where their brainstem is. I then say, "This is where you live and breathe. This is where your survival instincts come from." Clients often breathe a sigh of relief upon learning where their capacity to survive lives inside them.

• • •

Another Brainspotting technique I have developed is the called the Internal Brainscan. You can try it yourself now as I describe it.

As I explained earlier in this chapter, Brainspotting is based on the belief that the brain continually scans itself. In the Internal Brainscan approach, I encourage clients to experience the self-scan first hand, right in the moment. Here's what I say:

> Think of something that's bothering you, and then see—on
> a scale from zero (the least) to ten (the most)—how much

it's bothering you. Now notice where you are feeling it in your body.

Now I want you to close your eyes and literally look inside your brain and see what part of your brain is activated. Is it in the front, the middle, the back? Is it to the left or to the right? Is it up or down?

Now that you have located the activation, I want you to notice what it looks like. Notice its size and shape. Notice the color or darkness or lightness.

Now I want you to open your eyes and see where they want to go, as you hold the awareness of what you just saw or felt in your brain. Keep looking at that spot and simply observe wherever your mind goes.

After a few minutes of processing, I say:

I want you to close your eyes and go back to the location in your brain that you looked at before. Notice what it looks and feels like now. Has it changed?

If it has, notice how it has changed and how that change feels to you now. I want you to take your SUDS (zero to ten) again and see what it is now.

This entire step-by-step process is repeated over and over again. What's interesting about it is that the client finds not only an outside spot, but an inside spot as well. And clients often report feeling the connection between the spots. Perhaps this process is an actual harnessing of the brain's capacity to scan itself, not just a metaphoric one.

Clients are often amazed by what happens in a Brainspotting session or treatment. Many have been in therapy before and never gotten anything close to the results they get from Brainspotting. In just one session, clients can see things change in their experience of themselves and their lives. When they ask me, "How is this possible?" I always answer, "It's all brain stuff." And I believe it.

CHAPTER 10

Brainspotting and the Body

The Body Is Memory

R andi had originally come to me for treatment for her panic symptoms and pain syndrome. She grew up in a dysfunctional family where her parents fought day and night. At times the fighting turned violent. For the first five years of her life, Randi was much closer to her father than her mother. Her mother rejected her to the point of abusiveness. The words "You're ugly, you're stupid, and you're worthless" relentlessly spewed out of Mother's mouth at Randi. Her father was more maternal to Randi than her own mother. But that was until Randi turned five years old. Something changed, and it was probably a result of the escalation of Randi's father's drinking. First he became cold and aloof. Then he began to rage and become physically abusive with Randi. She never knew what hit her—literally. Randi tried to be the best daughter she could; in fact, she became a caretaker to both her parents. But being a "perfect" child didn't stop the daily onslaught.

No one knew of Randi's daily torment. Her parents were house devils and street angels. They were well-respected in the community.

Randi was seen as coming from an ideal family, when in truth, she lived in a private hell.

In her adolescence, she began to have panic attacks that seemed to come out of nowhere. She awoke in the middle of the night feeling like her chest was being crushed. Her anxiety would build throughout the day and crescendo at night. Randi went on to study education in college, and with grit and determination, somehow made it through. She was able to support herself with her teaching job and began to date. But the panic attacks never went away, and she struggled every day.

At age twenty-four, Randi started feeling pains in her legs. As the months passed, the pain intensified and spread to her back and her neck. She sought medical help and went from doctor to doctor. None of the medical experts were able to find the source of the pain or arrive at a definitive diagnosis. It was hypothesized that Randi might have fibromyalgia, neuropathy, reflex sympathetic dystrophy, or simply an unidentified pain disorder. Because of her history of panic disorder, more than a few of the doctors felt the pain might be psychological, and one even said it was just "in her head."

That doctor was insensitive, but not wrong. The pain that Randi felt was, in a sense, "in her head." It existed in her brain—and in her nervous system. Because our nervous systems encompass both the brain and the body, everything we feel in our bodies is, in fact, being felt in our brains. Our bodies and our brains are inseparable; they are an integrated unit. So when I refer to the body in this chapter, I am also referring to the brain.

We feel emotional pain in our bodies. Heartache is a clear illustration. Disease, injury, and pain are psychologically traumatizing as well, and the emotional trauma from physical conditions also resides in the nervous system. The physical and the psychological interact and are entwined with each other. At some level, physical and emotional experiences are indistinguishable. This doesn't mean that we can't have differential diagnoses of physical and psychological conditions. But it does mean that doctors need to be aware of the ever-present psychological resonance that accompanies physical illnesses. Psychotherapists need to be equally aware of the somatic issues that accompany all psychological conditions.

When Randi came to me for psychotherapy, it was not my role to fully diagnose her physical condition, as I am not a physician. But it was my responsibility to be mindful of the interplay between her panic and pain conditions, especially in the context of her traumatic history. I knew that by using Brainspotting, I would have a chance to reach where she was holding her emotional trauma in her nervous system, and I knew that doing so might reduce her body pain. Psychology is a reflection of physiology, and Brainspotting is a physiological approach with psychological consequences. Brainspotting shouldn't be used as a primary treatment for medical conditions, but when it is used to heal the emotional trauma of a physical condition, it can reduce the physical symptoms and help medical treatment to do its job.

• • •

In treating Randi with Brainspotting, I was curious how her symptoms, both psychological and physical, would respond. I took an extensive personal history, which included her family experiences and her psychological and medical history. I noticed that at times during this history-taking process, Randi would sob deeply, and at other times, she would talk in a flat, matter-of-fact way. She told me that her greatest trauma was not her mother's vicious verbal abuse, but the loss of her father's love, when he pulled away and turned against her. This is where we started the Brainspotting process. Because of Randi's traumatic history and because of her unexplained pain condition, I proceeded with caution. I used the full Resource Model, including the Body Resource and the Resource Spot, and One-Eye Brainspotting, starting on her Resource Eye (where her SUDS level was lower). I even guided Randi to look past the pointer, all the way to the wall (z axis), which helped her to feel less threatened. We monitored her body pain closely to make sure it wasn't exacerbated by the opening up of her painful memories. In the early sessions, I made sure Randi and I spoke throughout the process, so she would feel my presence and not become ungrounded.

When she brought up the pivotal memory where her father literally pushed her away, Randi gazed at the Brainspot on the wall like she was watching a video. Her eyes were wide open, and her pupils were powerfully dilated. She cried out repeatedly, "Daddy, what did I do wrong? What did I do wrong?" But the memories didn't stop there. Randi saw image after image of rejection and physical abuse by her father. She smelled the alcohol on his breath and cried out in pain as she felt his belt buckle hit her legs and back. And she saw her mother off to the side, egging Randi's father to "beat it out of her."

You might wonder what it was like for me to witness such a painful process. After decades as a therapist, I have learned to maintain an emotional distance while not being so detached that I lose empathic contact with clients. It's a strange balance, because I am simultaneously exposed to a person's horror and grief and to the miracle of a person in the process of healing in front of my eyes. In truth, if you really care, the vicarious exposure does accumulate in a therapist's system at a deeply unconscious level. Being a trauma therapist takes its toll and necessitates ongoing self-care.

Randi's Brainspotting process was long and arduous. Her physical abuse at the hands of her father continued until Randi was fifteen, when she went to live with an aunt. Month by month, the trauma processing gradually led to a reduction in physical pain, although the pain spiked up many times during and in between her sessions. We used the many forms of Brainspotting including Inside Window and Outside Window, One-Eye and Two-Eye, Gazespotting, and Z-Axis Brainspotting. It was all necessary to help release the body memories Randi carried, along with the panic that came from the terror she lived with, waiting for the next beating.

Gradually her body felt the physical pain less and less, which was a tremendous relief for her on all levels. But her pain relief plateaued at a SUDS level of three out of ten. Continued processing was unable to break through the barrier. We had processed the body memories of the assaults that had been stored in Randi's brain, but we had not processed out the emotional pain that was also held in her brain. She was still feeling the emotional pain coursing through the same sites where the physical pain from the beatings had been.

The remaining emotional pain sourced back to her mother's cruel rejection, which dated back to Randi's birth. You may recall that in the history-taking I did in the beginning of Randi's therapy, there were times when she became detached. These shutdowns came when she was talking about her mother. Randi believed that she had already handled the issues with her mother and that it was her father's betrayal and abuse that she couldn't get over. In truth, she had unconsciously buried, or dissociated, the emotional agony she'd felt during her mother's hateful diatribes. This cut-off, emotional pain was finding its expression in Randi's body.

So we started again at the beginning and used Brainspotting to locate the eye positions that revealed the detached memories from the first five years of Randi's life. We still relied heavily on the Resource Model to keep her from losing herself in her pain. It worked. As we continued with months of trauma memory processing, Randi realized that her physical and emotional pain were intertwined as a result of how her parents both treated her, together. For her first five years, her father didn't protect Randi from her mother, and the following years, Randi's mother not only didn't protect her from her father, but also provoked him into further beatings.

This deeper work had reduced her pain, but the pain still remained at a baseline level, with occasional spikes of discomfort. This lingering physical pain was finally released in latter months of Randi's treatment, in the form of rage and grief over what she had been through, emotionally and physically, and what she had lost in her childhood of suffering. By the end, Randi was pain free, except for the usual aches and pains we all go through.

The Brainspotting work was essential to Randi's healing. Talk therapy reaches only the areas of the brain that use language, not the areas where the deepest of emotions and body experience are held. Randi's trauma-based emotional and physical pain were inexorably intertwined in her nervous system. Both manifestations needed to be treated simultaneously if she was to be free of her body pain and emotional panic. With Brainspotting, the brain can focus, in a laser-like way, to find, hold in place, process, and release emotional and physical trauma held in the brain and felt in the body.

• • •

Brainspotting therapists are taught to have any client's medical condition fully checked out with the appropriate physicians. We never assume that Brainspotting is the cure for physical pain or illness, and we consult with clients' medical doctors when needed. But we have found that Brainspotting supports the treatment of physical ailments by reducing symptoms and promoting the healing process. In a significant number of situations, Brainspotting has successfully reduced, and at times eliminated, undiagnosable or intractable symptoms, including pain and fatigue. Brainspotting therapists never assume that something (a condition) is something, but we never assume it isn't something either. We cautiously, but optimistically, apply Brainspotting and see what happens. Brainspotting is a no-assumptions, phenomenological model that works from the uncertainty principle and relies on the therapist's attuned tracking of a client's processing.

• • •

Head trauma is another condition where I have used Brainspotting with interesting results, especially in cases where the trauma involved a loss of consciousness, as frequently happens in auto accidents and similar situations.

I have heard people, even experts, say, "They'll never get that memory back, and they're better off that way." That's not necessarily true, and that's not necessarily so. There are two kinds of amnesia: physically based and psychologically based. The latter is called dissociation. A car accident with a head injury, for example, is both a physical trauma to the brain and an emotional trauma to the brain. So the loss of memory that follows can be both physically and psychologically based, coming from both the physical and emotional traumas.

I discovered that memory loss had its roots in both physical and emotional traumas as I used Brainspotting with clients who had suffered head traumas from car accidents; I treated these clients the way I treated clients with PTSD. First, I ask the client, "What was the first moment you knew something bad was going to happen?" The answer usually is something like, "I saw the car cross the center divider, and I knew I couldn't avoid it." If there was memory loss due to a loss of consciousness, I ask for the last thing the person remembered before they lost their memory and the first thing they remember upon regaining consciousness.

We then find a Brainspot that goes along with the beginning of the accident or the moment the person lost consciousness. We take the SUDS level and locate where the activation is held in the body. Then we start the processing.

It is fascinating to watch, as the person usually processes the experience like any another nonaccident trauma. The processing goes sequentially through the event, from beginning to end, with images, sounds, emotions, and body experiences. I then guide the client to go back to the beginning and start again. Oftentimes the SUDS level has dropped, and trauma has begun to recede into the past.

Some of the brain-injury symptoms may have been reduced, and some of the amnesia may have lifted. Many times, clients have said things like, "I regained consciousness for a few minutes in the ambulance, and I'm just remembering it now." It's not unusual for a person to doubt their own memory experience, saying, "That couldn't have happened. I must be making it up." This is the same doubt I have heard many emotional-trauma survivors express when the veil of dissociation lifted in front of their eyes.

Please note that Brainspotting therapists know that human memory can be unreliable, so events need to be verified before they can be accepted as facts. By talking with family and friends, clients have been able to corroborate the details of events and conversations that the client recaptured during Brainspotting processing. On a few occasions, clients have been able to fully recall what had been assumed to be memory loss due to head trauma. Clients experience this recovery of memory as integration, as opposed to being forced to remember something they are better off forgetting. In these cases, as in Randi's, the emotional and physical traumas are tightly interwoven in the nervous system, so healing the psychological trauma helps heal the physical trauma as well.

I have worked with many members of the military returning from Iraq and Afghanistan who have been diagnosed with PTSD, mild to moderate traumatic brain injury (TBI), or both. Watching them bring home pieces of themselves that they had left behind, frozen in the combat zone, feels like watching a miracle unfold. It feels like a greater miracle to see blackouts and other brain-injury symptoms gently heal.

Brainspotting, along with other parallel methods, is on the forefront of brain-body work. Although we still don't understand exactly how these brain-based methods work, I feel we are approaching new vistas of healing by being able to access the brain with precision and hold it in place as it heals itself and the body.

CHAPTER 11

Brainspotting and Sports Performance
Rebuilding the Shattered Field of Dreams

have been an athlete and a sports fan since I was five or six years old. As a talk therapist, I occasionally worked with people on sports issues. I wasn't, however, able to make the connection between my athlete self and my therapist self.

This changed when, early in my EMDR days, I learned that EMDR was being applied to performance, particularly in sports. At the first EMDR conference I attended in 1994, I excitedly enrolled in a workshop on EMDR and performance. I sat through the entire seminar, waiting for the illuminating information from the two sports psychology experts who presented. I was disappointed when what was presented was pretty much boilerplate EMDR, with little unique and innovative application to sports performance. I later learned that the presenters were cognitive behavioral therapists, not attuned to the depth psychology approach I studied back in my psychoanalytic days. The presenters also said definitively that when "emotional problems came up" with their "performance" clients, they referred the clients to another EMDR therapist for "personal" work. When the personal issues were resolved, the performance work was resumed. In other words, the presenters separated performance issues from personal issues.

Even though I was new to both EMDR and performance work, this separation seemed clueless to me. I knew even back then that performance anxiety was personal anxiety expressed through the performance. I also knew that performance blocks were personal blocks of a dissociative nature. Dissociation comes from trauma, so performance blocks must come from trauma as well.

When I started doing EMDR with clients who had sports performance blocks and anxiety, I wasn't surprised that deeper traumatic experiences emerged. Many of these traumas occurred during the clients' athletic performances and during practice and preparation for the performances. Later I coined the term *sports trauma stress disorder* (STSD) for athletes to refer to these experiences. But many of the traumas were from early in life, and were the same kind of traumas I was seeing in my other clients. These early traumas were often what in psychotherapy are called *attachment issues.* This term refers to disruptions in our early attachments to our mother or other caretakers. These disruptions happen before we learn language and have thought, and so they can't be expressed or understood; they are just felt. It was readily apparent to me that performance is in the performer and the performer is a person. If you take the person out of the performance, you don't have much left, and any performance work you do will be limited in scope, duration, or effect.

I had good success with athletes using EMDR to address issues of sports traumas. My transition to Brainspotting helped me to be more focused and successful not only with my general therapy practice, but with my performance clients as well. In my further Brainspotting work with athletes, I made some discoveries that startled me.

• • •

I was working with Phil, a college catcher on a Division I (D-I) baseball team, on his throwing difficulties. Phil didn't have trouble throwing out a stealing baserunner or making any bang-bang (rapid) plays. These movements were all based on reflexive reactions and were not problematic for him. His difficulty was in the routine throwing of the ball back to the pitcher after each pitched ball. That's when he had time to "think about what he was doing." This loss of function is a most baffling affliction for an athlete. A pro golfer who can't drop a putt from four feet or closer is suffering a similar thing. It is known as "the yips," and athletes also call it "the beast," "the thing," or simply "it." The yips are feared to be contagious and so are not talked about by athletes or coaches. Accordingly, athletes believe it to be a rare affliction, while in truth, it is remarkably widespread across all sports, around the world. Athletes with the yips suffer in isolation, self-imposed and subtly imposed by teammates and coaching staffs.

Phil's throwing woes broke out early one spring season in his freshman year. A foul tip caught Phil directly between the seam in his right shoulder pad. His arm went numb down to his fingertips, which pulsed. Two innings later, Phil's toss-back after a pitch sailed over the pitcher's head. Luckily, no one was on base, and everyone, including Phil, laughed it off. Phil ceased laughing when he spiked the next toss-back into the ground five feet in front of home plate. On the following throw-back, Phil's hand locked in a "death grip" on the ball, and his arm seized up. Phil actually peered at the ball in his hand, feeling like he was looking at a foreign object. He literally froze and had to be removed from the game.

The coaches called it an injury, but one coach had suffered the yips earlier in his career and recognized it in Phil. The coach worked with Phil around his throwing mechanics, and they made gradual improvement. But Phil was never the same gifted catcher, and each time he went behind the plate, he felt increasing anxiety.

Phil went to see a sports psychologist who claimed a 100 percent cure rate for the yips. The psychologist used the traditional combination of visualization, relaxation exercises, cognitive behavioral "mental toughness" work, and hypnosis. Phil experienced slight improvement that was quickly lost. The psychologist gave Phil homework, which Phil did dutifully. Frustrated with Phil's lack of progress, the psychologist accused Phil of "not working the program." (I suppose that's how the sports psychologist attained his 100 percent cure rate: he dismissed any client who wasn't cured.) Phil never returned for sessions and was even more frustrated and discouraged. He considered quitting the game that he loved so much and carried such talent in.

Phil was referred to me by a family friend. By that point, he doubted that anything could help him.

In our first session, I took a brief history and then tried some initial Brainspotting to see how he would respond. I guided Phil to remember the first moment his yips arose. Three images came to him: the first was the ball he threw sailing over the pitcher's head, the second was him spiking the ball, and the third was being removed from the game. It was interesting, but not unusual, that he did not visualize being hit in the shoulder by the ball.

We started with the first image. Phil's SUDS level was eight, and not surprisingly, he felt it in his throwing shoulder. We found an Inside Window Brainspot, and Phil started processing. His processing immediately jumped back to being clipped on the shoulder by the foul tip. However, what followed caught me off guard. Phil's processing jumped from one sports injury to another. First was a shoulder injury catching when he was fifteen. Next was a broken hand at thirteen, followed by an elbow dislocation that same year. The most powerful injury that arose was one where Phil was knocked cold and suffered a severe concussion as a result of a collision at home plate when he was seventeen.

I suddenly realized that sports injuries are highly significant sports traumas. These sports traumas collect over time, only to emerge, and sometimes erupt, at a juncture that is neither anticipated nor understood. Thinking back, I must have intuitively understood this connection because of all the sports injuries I had experienced as a youngster.

My friends and did not play organized sports as most kids do now. We played pick-up sports that we organized in our own way. We decided whether we were going to play baseball, basketball, or football, and then we chose up sides. At times, my friends and I would organize and play against another group of kids from the neighborhood or against kids from other neighborhoods. It was Queens, New York, in the 1960s. It was all spontaneous and almost always seemed to work out. Even without formal Little League teams, the competition was fierce, and the play was rough and tumble. It was not unusual for someone to get injured, and I was no exception. We usually "shook it off" and "played through the pain." Occasionally someone went down and had to be carried off the field and even carried home. Hospital visits were rare, but not unheard of. I believe I received a number of concussions, and I remember acutely when I suffered a severe eye injury from being poked on the basketball court. I also broke my foot during a basketball game, but played on, hobbling until the game was over. Sports injuries are still accepted as natural in sports, even when it's children that are playing.

In treating other athletes following my work with Phil, I repeatedly observed how sports injuries were profound, cumulative sports traumas that interfered directly or indirectly with the athlete's performance. I had never read about this phenomenon in any literature on sports psychology or performance. In studying sports injuries as sports traumas, I came up with a conclusion about why they affect athletes so powerfully. A physical injury is a trauma to the nervous system that is felt in the site of the injury and stored in the brain. But a physical injury, especially during sports, is also a psychological injury to the nervous system. The simultaneity of the physical and psychological traumas leads them to be recorded together, and as such, interwoven and locked together in the brain and the body. At some level, I believe, the physical and emotional traumas become inexorably intertwined, especially as more traumas accumulate over time. In that way, the athlete's nervous system is like a minefield that possesses an ever-increasing number of land mines, just waiting to be stepped on. Brainspotting, with its laser-like use of the visual field to explore and locate traumas held in the brain and body, is an effective tool for both locating these mines and defusing them. But it is rarely a quick, easy process for athletes, and Phil was no exception.

Session after session, Phil and I processed his sports-injury traumas. There seemed to be a never-ending supply of his brain-body land mines. During the course of four months of treatment, Phil slowly, in fits and starts, regained his ability to naturally throw the ball back to the pitcher. But his treatment wasn't complete until he had Brainspotted two remaining life traumas.

When Phil was two years old, his mother had a complicated delivery with Phil's sister, Sara. Phil's mother was hospitalized for three weeks, and as far as he knew, his mother was gone forever. Coupled with that attachment interruption, Sara's arrival on the scene left Phil feeling shunted to the side, even when his mother returned. The second personal trauma Phil suffered was the death of his grandmother when he was six. Phil had been very close to her; she had taken care of him during his mother's absence following Sara's birth. With those traumas cleared, through a combination of Inside Window, Z-Axis, and Gazespotting, Phil was able to throw freely and without anxiety.

A few years after working with Phil, I had a chance to work with former New York Mets catcher Mackey Sasser. My work with him is chronicled in my book with Alan Goldberg, *This Is Your Brain on Sports*. Mackey's pro career was ended by the most famous case of throwing-back-to-the-pitcher yips. In fact, this throwing inhibition is known in the baseball world as Sasser Syndrome and Mackey Sasseritis. My work with Phil and other catchers prepared me for treating Mackey, who had a laundry list of sports injury traumas from childhood through his long pro ball career. He also had significant personal traumas in his childhood and adolescence. All it took was three extended Brainspotting sessions, and Mackey was able to freely throw during batting practice with the college team he coaches.

Mackey said the Brainspotting had also lifted a fifty-pound weight off his back.

• • •

Not every athlete has performance blocks of the magnitude of Phil and Mackey. But all athletes go through protracted slumps and losses of self-confidence. All athletes experience failure and humiliation, which is traumatic in itself. When any athlete opens up, they share the insecurities they carry regularly. During a slump, their insecurity only gets worse.

I have worked with athletes in numerous sports and have helped them to have shorter, shallower slumps. With Brainspotting, the athlete naturally flows back to their deep brain and away from the negative chatter in the conscious, thinking brain. The Resource Model is invaluable for helping athletes ground in their bodies and feel more relaxed when they perform. In our session, we identify the Resource Spot where the athlete feels calm and grounded. I guide them to use that spot in between sessions, not just when they are struggling, but also when they are feeling fine. The more the athlete works the spot, the more grounded they become in it. It is not uncommon for the athletes I have treated to look to that spot for a few seconds just before the moment of competition. All athletes look for every edge they can find, and this self-spotting provides it to them.

This leads to another application of Brainspotting in sports, which I call the Expansion Model of Brainspotting, which can help athletes expand and enhance their performance. (I prefer the term *performance expansion* to *peak performance,* as peak implies there are limits to performance enhancement.) The Expansion Model, in fact, applies to all types of performance, and to creativity and self-fulfillment as well. Brainspotting is not just a way of clearing away and healing emotional wounds, and a Brainspot doesn't just access where something negative is held in a person's system. There are Brainspots for virtually everything, including confidence, growth, insight, and self-love. A few of my spiritual clients have found a prayer spot and even a God spot. A Brainspot is simply an access or portal to the deeper neurobiology and body. Each person possesses perhaps an infinite number of points in their field of vision that correlate to the vastness of their inner experience.

There are two applications of the Brainspotting Expansion Model for sports. The first comes when an athlete's sports traumas are cleared and they are ready to process in a positive mode. As always, the body is the way we access any experience, either negative or positive. I like to guide athletes to return their awareness to the area of their body that held the negative activation the most during sessions. If an athlete is truly cleared, then this area of the body (often the chest, stomach, throat, head, or back) will feel either neutral or positive. All of the Brainspotting healing work we have done up to that point will have turned that area of body vulnerability into a Body Resource. Having turned a weakness into a strength, athletes feel great power and resilience. We then find the Brainspot that matches this newly created Body Resource and process from there. Oftentimes I observe athletes looking ahead, anticipating positive performances. Sometimes their brain returns to past failures and spontaneously rewrites the script in a positive way. This natural revision process is another remarkable example of how the brain heals itself.

The second application of Brainspotting in performance expansion is for athletes who are not struggling, but are looking solely to improve their performance. Brainspotting is not simply about removing blocks and alleviating anxiety; it is just as applicable to growth and expanding resilience. A baseball player who is hitting .280 can try to improve their batting average to .300. A golfer with an eight handicap can try to drop it to a six. A miler can try to shave seconds off their average run. My belief is that the greater the performance of an athlete (or any other performer), the higher their upside potential. If you talk to the greats in any sport, they will account for you, accurately, their areas of deficiency. Remember, all athletes are carrying the neural burden of countless accumulated sports traumas. The best performers in a sport have the genius of adaptation at the highest levels. Clear out the top athlete's traumas, and they have the potential to soar to new heights. Records in every sport fall all the time, even the ones deemed unbreakable.

When using Brainspotting for performance expansion with athletes who come simply to improve their performance, I start by identifying their strengths and finding Brainspots for them. The Expansion Model is like a supercharged version of the Resource Model; we find where the athletes feel the mastery and giftedness in their bodies and then match it with any type of Brainspot that flows with it. The processing that emerges from this expansion work is exciting and at times exhilarating. Occasionally an inhibition will surface and then process through. If the athlete chooses, after this positive processing, we can do some targeted work to identify and clear through any sports traumas (usually sports injuries). After this is accomplished, we shift back to the positive spot and body experience, and the expansion usually takes off from there.

• • •

Sports requires grace, agility, and inventiveness, all expressed mostly through body movement. Great athletes are often called creators, as they make new, unexpected things happen all the time. When the myriad blocks are cleared away, they invent that much more.

All of the same is true of artists, especially those in the performing arts. In the next chapter, I focus on how Brainspotting can identify and clear away blocks to creative expression in artists.

CHAPTER 12

Brainspotting and Creativity

All the World's a Stage

have coined the saying, "There is no healing without creativity, and there is no creativity without healing." The healing process of Brainspotting is highly creative, and Brainspotting can also unleash and expand creativity in artists.

As a therapeutic process, Brainspotting is not protocol driven; there are no steps or procedures that have to be followed. Anything predetermined interrupts and distracts the therapist's intuitive attunement to the client in the moment and impinges the client's creative healing process. Brainspotting works simultaneously with the right brain and the left brain, thus mirroring and integrating both the brain's artistic and scientific nature. Brainspotting parallels art in that it too incorporates form and structure, tools and technique, especially in the open tracking of the client's processing within the Dual Attunement Frame.

Survival, resilience, and recovery all require and reveal our creativity. Brainspotting accesses the genius of the deeper brain. In the Brainspotting healing process, I get to see how intuitive, inventive, and intelligent all human beings truly are. The processing I observe with clients, activated on and focused by a Brainspot, is deep, rapid, and unpredictable. I am always waiting for the surprise, and I am rarely disappointed. Scenes from different life events emerge as flipping images, only to morph into swirling emotions and fluid body sensations. Questions pop up in the client, only to be followed by cogent answers that seem to come out of nowhere. Or rather, it only seems like nowhere, because the answers come from the deeper, creative recesses of the brain that are usually inaccessible to conscious awareness. Somehow, in response to the processing, the client's SUDS level inexorably drops toward zero, with occasional spikes upward as new material emerges. This process parallels the creative process, where the artist receives and observes the flow of ideas that emerges from their deeper self.

I have worked with hundreds of artists from countless disciplines, including acting, singing, dancing, composing, writing, painting, drawing, and sculpting. I have used Brainspotting to help them with their personal problems as well as their creative issues. I have also developed Brainspotting as a method specifically for coaching actors. When using Brainspotting to help artists with creative expansion and for coaching within their particular art forms, I have observed that profound healing occurs simultaneously with the creative opening and deepening. I have actually come to believe that the baseline of creative enhancement is healing. In other words, "there is no healing without creativity, and there is no creativity without healing."

Many artists, running the gamut from actors to painters to writers, believe that if they are healed from their traumas, they will lose their creativity. This is an erroneous, superstitious notion. The truth is that trauma doesn't generate creativity; it inhibits creativity. Trauma doesn't grant access to experience; it blocks experience with reflexive barriers of dissociation. Artists can create from trauma, but their creative process accesses only a narrow bandwidth of woundedness. A canvas can be covered with jagged streaks of black and red, and an actor can represent a tortured soul. When Brainspotting heals the artist of their wounds, their spectrum of creativity widens dramatically. The painter can use all the colors on the palette, and the actor can bring nuance and hope to even the most tortured character. Trauma encapsulates artistry (literally in the brain), while Brainspotting liberates creativity to its exponential possibilities.

Some people mistakenly believe that Brainspots only locate trauma in the brain. There are, in fact, countless points in our field of vision that access any and all aspects of ourselves. Brainspots are access points for creativity as well as woundedness. Additionally, there are a variety of creativity Brainspots. An actor who also sings will likely have different Brainspots for connecting with their acting and singing abilities. A composer can derive words and music for the same song using different Brainspots. A writer who switches from comedy to drama will often have to switch their creative Brainspots. Oftentimes an artist is gifted in many different modes of creativity, and thus has and can benefit from accessing a variety of Brainspots.

• • •

Soren was in his mid-thirties when he first came to me for sessions. He had emigrated to the United States from his native Denmark at age twenty-two. He came to me to help unblock his creativity and overcome his deep feelings of inadequacy. As he unfolded his story, Soren gradually revealed his talents to me one by one. At the beginning of treatment, he was working as a lead dancer on Broadway. He couldn't help but be graceful, as it was simply in his nature. Then he shared with me that he was also an aspiring actor. Next he unveiled his singing abilities. He then shared that he was a playwright and had completed writing the play for a musical. Soren then let me in on the fact that he had written the words and lyrics for the musical as well.

My work with Soren progressed over time from Brainspotting trauma processing to creative expansion work. Soren was one of four siblings. His mother was a powerhouse who overshadowed and often belittled Soren's father. By extension, she communicated hostility towards all men as a gender. As far as Soren could tell, his mother didn't seem to notice that he was male. It felt to Soren like his mother was trying to draw him into her belief that men were crude and incompetent. This only sowed the seeds of his feelings of insecurity and inferiority. "I'm not good enough" became his mantra.

Teachers and coaches of artists can be demanding and critical to the point of being abusive. Soren's teachers were no exception, especially the head instructor of the dance academy that Soren attended throughout his teens. He was his teacher's pet, but somehow that role also made him the prime recipient of her scorn. Soren couldn't tell if she was pushing him hard because of his talent or his lack of it. Once, as an act of retribution, the teacher shut Soren out of the academy's annual performance. Instead of shining as the production's star, Soren watched it from the audience. Although he knew his banishment was capricious and unfair, he couldn't escape the ringing in his ears: "I'm not good enough." At the same time, somewhere deep inside, Soren knew he was not only good enough, but special.

It's not surprising that in addition to being highly creative, Soren was highly sensitive. Artists see the world differently than most of the population. In fact, some see a different universe than other people do. Their perceptions may take the form of images, sounds, movements, or concepts. Artists usually possess this intuitiveness from their earliest years. But when the creatively gifted share this awareness, it is not usually understood or well received by parents, teachers, siblings, and peers. As a result, creatively gifted people, starting in childhood, get wounded in their most treasured and yet most vulnerable area, their giftedness. Their giftedness draws both attention and scorn from other people. Such wounds are the unkindest cuts of all and the deepest ones as well. Abuse to one's area of giftedness and its expressions has a dual effect: it wounds the soul, and it lays down the foundation for creative anxiety and blocks. Throughout my decades of practice, my artist clients have uniformly shared that they suffered abuse because of their creative nature. "You don't know what you're talking about," "You're stupid," "You're crazy," "You're a trouble-maker," and the ubiquitous, "You're too sensitive" are epithets usually directed at the gifted. Likewise, Soren had crawled into a shell, believing he was inadequate.

In addition, artists, like athletes, are often physically injured doing their art. These injuries are well-known among dancers, who push their bodies to the point of agony in practice and performance. This process starts early in the career of child dancers and lasts a lifetime. Dancers perform at the nexus of art and athletics and are vulnerable to both sports and creative injuries. When an injury occurs during an important stage performance, it is compounded. Soren was not exempt from this cruel reality.

But dancers are not the only artists subject to physical injuries. Actors both use and abuse their bodies for the stage and the camera. For the film *Raging Bull,* Robert De Niro first whipped himself into incredible shape to portray boxer Jake LaMotta, then he gained fifty pounds to play the older LaMotta for the latter stages of the movie. Singer Idina Menzel, in her second-to-last performance of *Wicked* on Broadway, fell through a trap door and cracked her ribs. I once worked with a well-known film actor who suffered multiple concussions in the making of an action film. Then, when exposed to a strobe light, he actually went completely blind for two hours. Musicians often suffer repetitive motion and carpel tunnel injuries that can set back or end their careers. These same injuries befall graphic artists like sculptors and painters.

As these physical injuries are incurred during the artistic process with concurrent psychological injuries, the two are locked indecipherably together, just as they are with athletes. Movement and art are inseparable, and any inhibition to movement inhibits the creative process and infuses it with anxiety.

The most pernicious trauma that artists face is rejection. This applies to every art form. For every acceptance, there are hundreds, if not thousands, of rejections. It is a wonder any artist can survive and prevail through this phalanx of rejection. Auditions are often intentionally or inadvertently abusive. These "tryouts" can be something between a banishment and an execution. No matter how many times it happens, hearing "Next!" or "Thank you!" in the middle of a monologue is jarring and humiliating. Sometimes an actor or singer brings down the house with an amazing audition and doesn't receive the courtesy of a call informing them they were not chosen. Actors are uniformly told things like, "We like you, but your eyes are too close together" or "We don't like your shoulders." All too often, performers are left in a silent isolation chamber with no idea why they didn't book the part. Even when they do get the role, actors, singers, and dancers are frequently screamed at and humiliated by abusive directors. Some performers are fired capriciously in rehearsal or on set. I have worked with graphic artists who have had their favorite works stolen or defaced.

Finally, the term *starving artist* accurately reflects how some of the most gifted artists and performers live on subsistence incomes. The goal in acting is not to become a star; it is to become a "working actor." This phrase means simply to be able to support oneself from one's acting. With an office in Manhattan, I am privileged to do Brainspotting with many of the artists who flock to the city as a mecca. I often lower my fee, at times drastically, for them; it's my way of being a patron of the arts.

It can take many sessions of Brainspotting to heal the core wounds of artists. Thus was the case with my work with Soren. Fortunately, he was what I call a "high responder" to Brainspotting. Ensconced on any form of Brainspot, and listening to BioLateral Sound through a pair of headphones, Soren was off to the races. His processing was as amazing as his artistry. I wish I could have seen the trauma-to-healing images in his head that eluded his description. Sometimes I simply watched the shifting phases of emotion, realization, and release on Soren's face with wonderment. The creatively gifted heal in the most creative of ways. Artists have amazing neural pathways, formed by genetics and the constant development of their craft.

One by one, Soren's traumas released as he healed. It was extremely important to him that I understood the intricate creativity that had been so wounded throughout his life. Not only didn't I judge anything, but I also attuned to his giftedness. I may have been the first person to realize how brilliant he was and reflect that recognition to him. While holding the pointer to focus his gaze, I was dazzled to discover new aspects of his talent. I have seen some therapists intimidated or even diminished by clients with special abilities. For me, working with Soren was like a trip to the ultimate Disneyland. It is ideal when a creatively gifted therapist works with a creatively gifted client.

Gradually our work morphed from emotional healing to performance expansion work. First, Soren brought in an audition monologue that he wanted to work on to improve his acting. I had him read through the monologue once, and then I helped him to find the "character spot." Guiding Soren with Inside Window Brainspotting, I moved the pointer first to the right, then to the middle, then to the left, followed by above and below eye level. I asked, "Where do you feel him (the character) the most?" Soren pointed left and up, and I asked, "Where do you feel him in your body the most?" Soren, without words, put his hand on his heart. I asked Soren, "What line from the monologue pops into your head now?" And he answered, "I never knew."

I guided Soren to observe his processing with the notion that it was the character (named Charles) who was processing, not himself, the actor. Soren had a series of memories that flashed by with deep emotional and body resonance. There was a twist, however. The memories were not Soren's, but those of Charles. As his gaze stayed locked on the Brainspot, sights, sounds, and smells all flashed in front of Soren. They seemed to come out of nowhere, but they were all organic to Charles and the monologue. Actors spend hours and days trying to create and connect with characters, and Soren was doing it in almost no time.

After fifteen minutes, he recited the monologue. Chills ran up my spine as Soren embodied the character right in my office. Exhilarated, Soren said, "I blew myself away!"

But the process wasn't over. When you take an actor so deeply into character, it is unwise to leave him there. So we found the Soren spot, or self-spot, that helped him process out of Charles and back into himself. Soren said, "I want to hold onto a bit of Charles for the audition." I asked Soren, "Where in your body do you want to hold on to Charles?" Soren lifted his left hand, and we found the Brainspot that guided the transfer to occur. Charles slowly exited Soren's body and drained gently into Soren's left hand.

I had a final suggestion to Soren: "Just before your audition, place your left hand back on your heart and look to the left and up and locate the character spot we worked with today."

Soren followed my instructions and killed at the audition. He got the part.

• • •

The acting session was the beginning of Soren's work with me on all aspects of his creative process. One day he came in with a tape recorder and said, "I want to work on a song." I knew Soren was taking singing lessons, but his voice amazed me. Then he asked, "Can you help me with this?" I thought to myself, "What could I do to make his song better?"

Through my work with artists I have discovered that creativity is exponential. It is remarkable that the higher you go, the further your upside potential becomes. During the session, Soren's vocal resonance and emotional connection to his song increased.

Another session he started by saying, "I'm working on a dance routine, and I'm stuck in one place." We went out to my waiting room, for more space, with my pointer and went to work. I got to see another side of Soren's giftedness, and it was exhilarating. He showed me the move he was struggling with, and it looked fine to me. But he knew where the problem was, so we found the Brainspot that identified where he felt blocked. We worked it through, literally step by step. Soren almost flew across my waiting room when we were done.

In the final chapter of the story, Soren came into my office with the script of a play. He said, "I wrote this," as he handed it to me. "Would you read this for me?" I had done script-consultant work on films and plays before to ensure that the stories were psychologically sound. So I took the script and answered, "Sure." Soren told me that he had written the entire play listening to my BioLateral CDs. The play was about a multitalented entertainer, and I saw how Soren infused himself into the lead character.

In reading his play, I was struck by two things: First, Soren had a wicked sense of humor that he had never shared with me before. Second, his written English, Soren's second language, was impeccable—not one grammatical error, not one misspelling, excellent use of the American idiom. It was perfect, which is almost impossible for a non-native speaker. Soren's play, which included a score that he had composed and lyrics that he had written, was incredible. I was able to make a few helpful notes on the psychology of the main character, and Soren was more than appreciative.

Soren had a crucial decision to make about who should direct his play. He was considering doing it himself, but knew that financial backers would want to bring in a name director. I took out my pointer and said, "Let's find your decision spot." The Brainspot was dead center. Soren stared down the spot for ten minutes, then closed his eyes. I could see that he was still staring at the same spot inside. Soren went for ten more minutes as I waited patiently.

Finally he opened his eyes and said, "I'm directing it." Soren also decided to produce and choreograph his play as well, and he never looked back.

We have continued Brainspotting on every creative and personal issue that has emerged in the process of making his play a reality.

Occasionally, under duress, Soren has a temporary lapse into insecurity. It doesn't take much Brainspotting, and he is back on track. He has staged a major workshop of his play and is now in the process of raising the copious amount of money required to stage a Broadway musical. Soren's mantra is no longer, "I'm not good enough." His mantra has evolved into, "I'm a proud artist."

• • •

I have designed Brainspotting to be an open, creative model. On a Brainspot, the therapist tracks the client's intuitive, in-the-moment healing process. This creative component makes Brainspotting a natural fit for both treating artists and expanding their creative potential. I take the Brainspotting techniques that work in session with an artist and teach the artist to use these tools outside of the office, on their own. In the next chapter, I will show you how to use your field of vision to do some self-Brainspotting on your own.

CHAPTER 13

Self-Brainspotting

Harnessing Your Visual Field

P eople ask me all the time, "Can you do Brainspotting on yourself?" I usually answer, "You're doing it right now." I then explain that by looking at me, the questioner has established an eye position that correlates with activation in discrete areas of their brain. I describe how Brainspotting is deeply intuitive, and for the most part, unconscious.

We do self-Brainspotting all day, every day. When we gain awareness of how we are affected by where we look, we can harness this natural phenomenon. Knowing that you are accessing information based on where you are looking helps you understand yourself and use eye positions consciously. In fact, you are doing so now as you are reading this sentence. Be aware of that. Track your internal process for a minute as you look at these words, and see where it takes you.

I didn't invent the power of where we look; I simply noticed it. In truth, I knew it all along, just like everyone else does, deep within my unconscious perception. But I consciously recognized the power of an eye position when I saw my client Karen's eyes wobble and I held my finger steady at the spot she was looking at when that occurred. The fact that Karen had no idea that her eyes were wobbling points to the reality that no one can do by themselves what they can do with the help of a therapist, especially with Brainspotting. Throughout this book, I have referred to the Dual Attunement Frame—where the therapist attunes to the client on both a relational and neurological basis—as the power of Brainspotting. You can't observe yourself from the outside, so you can't do dual attunement flying solo.

It is also unwise to try to do deep trauma work by yourself, because you never know what you might unearth. When things emerge unexpectedly in a Brainspotting session, chances are that the therapist has seen the same things many times before and knows quite well how to help you to ground and stabilize. Deep memories and feelings do emerge for us periodically, and with help and time, we are usually able to process them and rebalance.

While several Brainspotting models and techniques require the guidance of a trained Brainspotting therapist, there are aspects of Brainspotting you can use on your own, to help you feel calmer and more grounded, to help your sleep, and to enhance your creativity or performance ability. In this chapter, I share a variety of Brainspotting self-use tools.

• • •

The first tool is the easiest to use. In fact, I used it as I was writing this book. It is BioLateral Sound, which moves sound gently back and forth from ear to ear. (See Chapter 3 for how I developed BioLateral Sound and use it in Brainspotting sessions with clients.)

The BioLateral Sound CDs and downloadable music files are programmed to phase-shift, or move left and right, gentle healing music and nature sounds. They work in two ways at the same time. First, they activate the parasympathetic, or calming, nervous system. This helps to relax our bodies and brains, which also puts us in a state for expanded performance. Second, by moving the sound from one ear to the other and back again, the sound alternatingly stimulates the left and right brains. This stimulation promotes left-right brain communication, integration, and harmony. BioLateral Sound is highly effective when used in Brainspotting sessions, but it is also valuable for self-use.

Self-use of BioLateral Sound has many applications. First, as noted, it promotes brain calming and body relaxation. If you are tense or anxious, listening to BioLateral Sound will help you calm down. If you are in a calm state already, you will likely find your way into an even calmer state. This soothing effect varies from person to person and situation to situation. Some people respond quickly, while others take longer. Being patient with yourself is always a good idea, so when you listen to the sound, give yourself time and space and take off your expectations. Relaxation doesn't come on command; it comes naturally, oftentimes when you don't notice it. The conscious brain doesn't calm down the deeper brain; it is the other way around. Remember, the deeper brain is where we live and breathe.

Many people find that BioLateral Sound helps them to fall into a restful sleep. That makes sense because it promotes relaxation and relaxation promotes sleep. It doesn't usually cure chronic insomnia, as sleep disturbance has many causes, some profound and others physical. But many people who have difficulty falling asleep find that BioLateral Sound helps when combined with other good sleep habits, like restricting caffeine intake, following a regular sleep schedule, and giving oneself a restful period of time before bed. It is a good idea to first use BioLateral Sound for relaxation during the day before trying it before sleep.

When you first use BioLateral Sound, you may experience a temporary increase in your activation. Why? Because it brings out whatever is on your mind, just below the surface. If something is bothering you, it may need to come out before you can feel calmer or grounded. The immediate activation is usually followed by a sense of release and relief. So try BioLateral Sound during the day first instead of just before bedtime. This will prevent the small possibility of getting activated and having your sleep interrupted.

You can listen to BioLateral Sound for relaxation or anxiety reduction while you are inactive or while you're involved in an activity. When used during activity, BioLateral Sound also begins to provide performance or creativity expansion. Students have reported that their study and test preparation improved while they were listening to it. Many actors I have worked with listen to BioLateral Sound right before they go onstage or in front of the camera. The actors reported that the sound helped open their creativity, get them deeper into character, and ground them. Two painters who have seen me for therapy always listen to BioLateral Sound through headphones while applying paint to canvas.

The beauty of using BioLateral Sound is that you don't have to do anything for it to work. The moving sound goes directly into your ears and travels into your deep brain and down into the body. It appears to work with the vagus nerve, the centerpiece of the parasympathetic (calming) nervous system, which runs from the brain directly to the heart, digestive, and respiratory systems. The vagus nerve lets us know we are safe from threat, so we can calm and slow down and let our attention go to our internal environment. This vagal response is simultaneously grounding and opening, supporting both relaxation and expanded performance and creativity.

See the resources section at the end of the book for where and how to order BioLateral Sound CDs and downloadable music files.

● ● ●

Here are three more tools for self-Brainspotting. The first is an exercise that utilizes the Body Resource from the Resource Model. It uses focused mindfulness with the Body Resource for the purposes of relaxation, clearing, and centering. For more specific problem-solving, self-healing, or performance expansion, use exercises 2 and 3, self-use variations of Gazespotting and Inside Window Brainspotting.

EXERCISE 1 FINDING AND USING YOUR BODY RESOURCE

This self-use exercise uses the Body Resource, the foundation of the Resource Model of Brainspotting. Chapter 4 has all the background information you need to understand the Body Resource, but simply put, it is the place in your body where you feel the calmest and most grounded.

Step 1: Find your Body Resource. The simple way to find your Body Resource is to slowly scan your body, from head to toe, for the place where you feel calm or grounded. It may be a large area, like your chest or your back, or an area as small as a coin behind your knee or on the bottom of your foot. Trust your instincts. You may find this place quickly, or it may take a while. Either way, be patient and gentle with yourself.

Also remember that your Body Resource corresponds to an area in your brain that is actually feeling the calm groundedness. It may help you further to imagine or visualize where that spot is in your brain. See the Internal Brainscan directions in Chapter 9 for guidance for how to find that internal spot.

Step 2: Do additional calming and grounding. First, if you are sitting, feel your feet in contact with the floor. You can either press your feet gently on the ground or shift them around. Be aware that as you are feeling your feet in contact with the floor, so is your brain. Next, be aware of the chair holding and supporting your body. (If you are lying down, be aware of the bed or floor supporting you.) Grounding ourselves in this literal way enables us to feel more emotionally grounded. It's how the brain and body work together all the time.

If you now feel sufficiently grounded, you can skip ahead to step 3. If you need additional calming or grounding before moving ahead, here are two sure-fire ways of accomplishing it.

The first is so simple it's almost silly. All you have to do is listen to your breathing. Don't try to slow or alter your breathing in any way; that works against the exercise. Just listen as you breathe in, and listen as you breathe out. Be aware that as you breathe in, you are inhaling oxygen that replenishes your body down to a cellular level. And know that as you breathe out you are exhaling carbon dioxide and thus cleansing your body down to a cellular level.

Breathing is controlled by the autonomic nervous system in our brainstem. We don't have to be taught how to breathe; it is an intuitive action that we do from birth. As you listen to yourself breathe, you are observing your brainstem at work for you. As you listen to the rhythm of your breathing, your breathing gradually self-regulates, which is calming in and of itself.

To continue to help yourself ground while watching your breath, take the fingers of one of your hands and place them gently on the area where the back of your head meets your neck. You are feeling just where your brainstem runs from your brain down into your spine. This is where we live and breathe. When you touch this spot as you listen to your breathing, you will connect with yourself and feel even more deeply grounded.

A second way to augment your calming and grounding is to let one of your hands spontaneously and slowly rise a bit and gently take hold of the other hand. Guide the holding hand to gently support the opposite hand. When you are ready, let the holding hand gently caress the held hand. Notice how calming and supportive this feels. After a while, if it feels natural, switch and let the held hand become the holding hand and do the caressing to other hand. This technique literally gets the right and left sides of your brain to soothe each other.

Now that you have located your Body Resource and given yourself additional calming and grounding, if necessary, you can shift into the focused-mindfulness phase.

Step 3: Processing with focused mindfulness. Brainspotting makes full use of mindfulness in the processing that happens after you setup and locate the Brainspot. If you are knowledgeable about mindfulness meditation, you will need little instruction here, except for starting and occasionally returning to awareness of your Body Resource. For those not familiar with mindfulness meditation, it is actually quite simple to combine it with the Body Resource.

Your Body Resource is where you start, where you occasionally return for regrounding, and where you finish. In between is the focused-mindfulness processing. The key is that this mindfulness is not directed. As with most Brainspotting, the more unguided it is, the better. As you stay aware of where you feel calm and grounded in your body, just observe, without expectation or judgment, wherever your mind goes. It may jump around to things that seem unrelated or just stay in one place for a while. Memories, thoughts, emotions, or body sensations may come and go. If what comes up seems random or inexplicable, don't fall into the trap of doubting the process. Your conscious observer brain is simply watching the processes of your deeper, unconscious brain. The key is to trust your instincts. I also like to say, "Observe with curiosity."

Allow this focused mindfulness to continue for about one minute before checking back with your Body Resource. Then start again, this time letting the focused mindfulness go on for three to five minutes before checking back. As the process continues, you will find your own rhythm and timing. Some people like to check back regularly on their Body Resource; some will wander for fifteen to twenty minutes before regrounding.

You can do this simple Body Resource processing for any period of time. Use the time you have, whether it is brief or more lengthy. The more you repeatedly use the exercise, the more benefit you will get, as its effects are cumulative. You will need to sit in a comfortable, nondistracting place for optimal effectiveness.

EXERCISE 2 SELF-GAZESPOTTING

This exercise uses our natural tendency to gaze in a direction that correlates to the position in the brain where we are holding an experience. Chapter 5 outlines in detail how Gazespotting works. This exercise will be enhanced if you combine it with listening to Bio-Lateral Sound, although you can do the steps effectively without it.

Self-Gazespotting starts with the Body Resource, so you will need to retrace the steps of exercise 1, "Finding and Using Your Body Resource," before proceeding.

Step 1: Locate a Gazespot. Once you have located or developed your Body Resource, you are ready to begin. Shift your awareness to this calm, grounded place in your body and just stay with it for five to fifteen seconds. During or after this time period, you may notice that your eyes have shifted to and fixated on something in your field of vision. This is your Gazespot. If your eyes don't shift immediately, you probably need more time. Just continue focusing on your Body Resource and let your mind wander for a while. Before you realize it consciously, you will be gazing at an unconsciously chosen spot, or Gazespot.

Some people naturally close their eyes when they go to their Body Resource. If that happens with you, notice that you are actually looking in a direction, even with your eyes shut. When you open your eyes, maintain that eye position and see what it aligns with in your visual field.

Step 2: Prepare to process. When you have your Gazespot, you are ready to start processing off that spot. You may choose to focus on something specific, like a speech you have to give or a relationship you're involved in, or you may leave the field of exploration open.

Whatever you choose to address, just think about it for a while as you focus on the Gazespot. Reviewing the issue while focusing on the spot serves to activate you around the issue, which also activates the areas of your brain that are holding the experience. Give a SUDS number to the level of your activation. The SUDS is from zero to ten, where no activation is zero and ten is the highest it can be. The SUDS will let you know where you are at in the process when you check back on it. I don't want you to look for the activation in your body now; that is for the in-session Brainspotting work.

Continuing to look at the Gazespot, return your awareness to your Body Resource. Remember, your Body Resource is just your starting point. You are not supposed to maintain your conscious awareness on the Body Resource, as your thoughts are meant to wander wherever they go. It is only your stare at the Gazespot that remains fixed through this exercise.

Step 3: Process with focused mindfulness. Now that you have completed your set-up, you are ready for the focused-mindfulness processing. This is the same as step 3 in exercise 1, except now the processing is occurring while you are focused on an issue and a Gazespot. Accordingly, the processing is usually more precise and specific.

The goal here is to just see where things go inside, without expectations. Trust that your deeper brain is wired to know how to process experiences and lead itself to solutions and balance. So do not try to preordain your destination, as you likely will not get there. Trust that wherever you go and wherever you arrive is where you need to be.

Every once in a while, check back on the original issue and take your SUDS level to keep track of where you are at in the process. Once you check your SUDS, simply shift your awareness back to your Body Resource (while you're still looking at the Gazespot), but don't try to stay focused on the Body Resource, as again it is merely a starting place that you return to occasionally.

The goal of this self-Gazespotting exercise is not to attain a zero SUDS level. That may or may not happen. What is important is giving your deeper brain-body system a chance to work on the issue and to process ahead. If you have open-ended time, you can intuitively sense when to end the processing. It may also help to set a predetermined amount of time and finish when you reach that time. You can always come back and work on the issue at a later juncture. But remember, the processing doesn't stop when the exercise does. Our brains are processing all the time, so it's not unusual for yours to keep processing for minutes and hours after you finish the self-Gazespotting.

EXERCISE 3 SELF–INSIDE WINDOW BRAINSPOTTING

Outside Window Brainspotting requires someone to be watching your eyes and face for reflexive responses on various eye positions. Because you simply can't be the watcher and the watched at the same time, you cannot do Outside Window on your own. But with Inside Window Brainspotting, the eye position is determined by your self-observation of your body cues. You can certainly find the visual locations where you feel a body response on your own.

Self-Brainspotting, as outlined in this chapter, uses the Body Resource from Resource Model. So we find the Inside Window Brainspot by determining where we feel the Body Resource the most. For that, go back to exercise 1, which tells you how to find a Body Resource.

When you have found the calm, grounded location in your body, you are ready to find the Inside Window Brainspot. This eye position is simply where you feel the presence of, or the connection to, your Body Resource the most. It doesn't matter whether you start on the left or right first, but I will illustrate by starting on the left.

Look at something in the room to your left and at eye level. See how your Body Resource responds as you gaze there for about ten seconds. Now look at something straight ahead and reflect for another ten seconds on how your Body Resource feels. Now look to an object to your right, at eye level, and reflect again on your Body Resource. Choose between left, middle, and right for where you feel your Body Resource the most.

Once you have determined where the spot is horizontally, or on the x axis, you are ready to proceed vertically on the y axis. From the x axis position (left, middle, or right) where you feel the Body Resource the most, look directly up, above eye level. Gaze there for ten seconds. Now go back to eye level and do the same. Then look directly down for ten seconds. See where on the y axis you most feel the presence of, or connection to, the calm, groundedness in your body.

Once you have located your Inside Window Brainspot, you are ready to proceed ahead. For instructions on the set-up process and focused mindfulness, return to steps 2 and 3 in exercise 2.

• • •

It is helpful to remember that we are self-spotting all the time, even with our eyes closed. Self-spotting is how we orient ourselves in space and time, both in our outside environment and our inside environment. This orienting process is rarely obvious, as it is determined by our deep brain-body. The next time you find yourself staring at a spot, don't think what you're doing is strange or random. Keep looking at that spot with the conscious awareness that there is something there for you. Then see what delivers itself to you.

CHAPTER 14

Brainspotting as an International Phenomenon

Around the World with Brainspotting

W hen I discovered Brainspotting in 2003, my first thought was that I stumbled onto a new, unique, powerful tool. After a month of using Brainspotting along with my colleagues, my second thought was that I wanted to develop a training program for Brainspotting. The third thought quickly followed: "Brainspotting is going to be an international, not just an American, phenomenon." It is now ten years later, and there are over six thousand therapists trained in Brainspotting, more than half of them outside the United States. I have trained twenty-one Brainspotting trainers: six are in the United States, four are in South America, ten are in Europe, and one is in the Middle East. And Brainspotting has so far been taught in six languages: English, Spanish, Portuguese, German, Dutch, and Hebrew.

Language and culture are essential parts of our identity and self-experience. Both language and culture are embedded in our brains, perhaps in our DNA. In the United States, most people speak only English, although this is changing as we become increasingly multicultural. In Europe, people tend to speak more than one language, and English is often the second tongue. Some Europeans speak five or more languages. Each language has its own idioms and nuances that are often untranslatable; they come more from the intuitive right brain than the informational left brain. Culture is highly linked to language, but comprises many other aspects. Family, community, customs, food, music, and much more are rich examples of dynamics that vary from culture to culture.

Brainspotting, with its direct access to the deeper brain and the body, is easily translatable to different cultures and languages. The Brainspotting therapist, in the context of the Dual Attunement Frame, is open and responsive to any and all client communications or reactions. With the no-assumptions model and uncertainty principle, the Brainspotting therapist follows the client wherever they go, just trying to stay in the tail of the comet. If the Brainspotting therapist misses a cultural or linguistic cue, it doesn't matter as long as the therapist keeps following the client with open curiosity. The open, integrative model of Brainspotting lends itself to attuning to clients of different backgrounds and languages.

Brainspotting associations are forming around the world. It won't be long before we hold our first international Brainspotting conference. It may be in the United States, or it may be in either Europe or South America. Whatever the locale, the vibrant mélange of the expanding Brainspotting community worldwide will be expressed at this gathering. The different languages in the Brainspotting universe are not a cacophony, but a harmony. What makes us different is also what makes us one.

• • •

From early on, I wanted Brainspotting to not be about me, but to outgrow me. The development of the international Brainspotting community is my greatest achievement with Brainspotting. I am often asked how I made Brainspotting such an international phenomenon. My answer is that I was already teaching outside the United States when I discovered Brainspotting. I had connections to other countries and professional friends in each one of them who would support my efforts to spread Brainspotting around the world.

When I'm asked why I felt it was so important to bring Brainspotting to other countries, I explain that I became an international person when I was seven years old. Accordingly, I don't think that the United States is the only country in the world or more important than other nations. I feel myself to be both a citizen of my country and a citizen of the world. So I have a strong point of view compelling me to reach out to therapists of other countries.

When I was seven, my parents took my sister, Debbie, and me on a four-month trip to Europe and the Middle East. My father was embarking on an international lecture tour, and my parents decided to make it a family adventure. We traveled to England and back by ocean liner, a week's journey in each direction. During our trip we visited the United Kingdom, the Netherlands, Belgium, France, Italy, Switzerland, Austria, Yugoslavia, Greece, Turkey, and Israel. Interestingly, Brainspotting trainings have already been conducted in ten of these eleven countries.

My parents didn't drive, so we traveled everywhere on Europe's remarkable train system. I have clear memories of gazing through train windows at the farms, forests, villages, mountains, and the tunnels under the Alps. But most of all I remember the people. My father had friends in every country, which was certainly a mark of the man. Some of his friends were rabbis; others were educators, writers, and artists. They were all fascinating characters. Many of my dad's friends had families with children, so my sister and I had playmates throughout the trip. When the other children didn't speak English, we always shared the common language of play. Even at age seven, I perceived both the commonalities and the differences among people. It was invigorating to experience, both the familiar and the foreign.

I don't know if it was my parent's conscious intention, but they helped develop me into an international person. They made the differences among people exciting instead of frightening, and they embodied this openness with their actions. I have a hard time understanding xenophobia, as the "other" is always fascinating to me. In my core, I know that the multiethnic fabric of the United States is what makes it great. I have heard that in my hometown of New York City as many as eight hundred languages are spoken.

My first opportunities to teach outside the United States came in the late 1990s, when I taught Natural Flow EMDR workshops in London and the Netherlands. It was thrilling to be back in Europe, not as a child, not as a tourist, but as an expert in my field. All the cultural enrichment from my youth buoyed me and enhanced my performance and my experience. I began building a network of international friends that would develop over the years and later support my efforts to bring Brainspotting around the world. Within a year after teaching in Europe, I was teaching Natural Flow EMDR in Argentina and Israel. A dear friend and EMDR trainer, Maria Elena Aduriz, brought me to Buenos Aires. The therapists I taught there were top-notch, equal to the finest in New York. All of South America, but Argentina in particular, has a long, rich history of psychoanalytic study and development. I have read that Argentina has more psychologists per capita than any country in the world.

It was a unique thrill to return to Israel to teach. I have traveled to Israel ten times throughout my life. The Natural Flow EMDR training was organized by my dear friend, Fran Yoeli. I experienced deep feelings while presenting in Israel, both about information I shared with the trainees and about teaching in my second home, a country that was so beloved by my father. I even attempted to speak some Hebrew, my second language, and was surprised how well my vocabulary held up.

• • •

In 2004, a year after my discovery, I gave the first three Brainspotting trainings in the United States: in Boston, New York City, and Chicago. You never know how a newly developed training is going to go until you give it. Fortunately, the trainings went well. Since then, I have given almost one hundred Brainspotting trainings. The original two-day Brainspotting training became the introductory Phase 1, and I taught it as I developed the advanced Phase 2 training. It is significant that I gave the first Phase 2 Brainspotting trainings in Berlin, not a US city; it reflected that Brainspotting was established to be an international therapy method.

The first international Brainspotting training was held in Buenos Aires in 2005, with translation into Spanish, and the first European Brainspotting training was held in Berlin six months later. These trainings led to the establishment of the first significant international Brainspotting communities, and both still exist today in South America and Europe. Brainspotting began spreading to new countries and therapists without my direct involvement. This was a milestone in the worldwide movement of Brainspotting.

Soon after the first Brainspotting training in Germany, Fran Yoeli organized the first Brainspotting training in Israel. The response was excellent, and the Brainspotting community in Israel was born. Its development exceeded my wildest expectations. I carry sadness that my father didn't live to see Brainspotting in Israel, as he was a passionate Zionist. But I am glad my mom lived long enough to see me bring Brainspotting to Israel and around the world. Fran has since kept up the pioneering spirit by conducting the first Brainspotting training in Greece in 2011.

The story of international Brainspotting took a crucial turn when Maria Elena Aduriz introduced me to her close friend Esly Carvalho, the leader of EMDR in Brazil. Esly was one of the pioneers of the method psychodrama not only in Brazil, but also throughout South America. Esly organized the first Brazilian Brainspotting training in 2007. After that, she not only brought me back to Brazil repeatedly, but she also took me to other countries, starting a remarkable domino effect. She first insisted that Santiago Jacome, the leader of EMDR in Ecuador, bring me in to do a Brainspotting training in Quito. We have since given numerous trainings in Ecuador, and Esly translated each one for me. (She is fluent in English and Spanish, as well as Portuguese.) A strong Brainspotting community now exists in Ecuador, and Santiago and Glenda Villamarin have been established as trainers there. In recent years, Santiago has traveled twice to Chile to give Brainspotting trainings.

Esly's reputation as an EMDR trainer and expert extended to Portugal and Spain, where she helped pioneer EMDR communities. Through Esly's connections, Margarida Couto, now a Brainspotting trainer, brought me in to do trainings in Lisbon, again translated by the indefatigable Esly. Portugal, despite its small size, was the first country to establish an official national Brainspotting association.

The next stop was Spain, where Esly connected me with Mario Salvador, a European leader in the fields of transactional analysis and integrative psychotherapy. I was hoping that a man of Mario's stature would become a Brainspotting supporter, and I was honored when he did. Esly again translated the first training in Lugo. With Mario leading the way, the Spanish Brainspotting community has become one of the strongest ones on the continent.

The second-generation Brainspotting stories continue, as Mario brought it to Romania, where he already had strong connections. There is now a well-established Romanian Brainspotting community (Mario has returned repeatedly) that I have had no direct connection with as yet. The same is true in Slovenia, where Mario has also recently brought in Brainspotting.

I may have started Brainspotting, but as I'd hoped, it is has far outgrown me. The fact that Brainspotting continues to be brought to new countries by trainers other than me is proof positive that Brainspotting has grown well beyond me and is the best sign of a job well done on my part. Meanwhile, I am continuing to expand Brainspotting's international reach.

In 2009, I traveled all the way to Australia and helped establish a new Brainspotting community there with Roby Abeles. In 2012, I conducted trainings in the United Kingdom with Philip Dutton and the Netherlands with Marie-Jose Boon. Scandinavia is now on the horizon, as Norwegian and Swedish Brainspotting therapists trained in other parts of Europe bring it back to their native countries. As of 2012, we have yet to conduct a training in France, but we have some feelers there.

• • •

The human brain is a reflection of our planet. The brain is made up of regions, and each region is composed of billions of brain cells. All these neurons are networked together by one quadrillion connections. The world has approximately two hundred countries and seven billion people. We all come from a common ancestor. With today's technology, we can communicate with anyone, at any time, around the globe. It is natural that Brainspotting is an international phenomenon. As varied as humans can be, our brains are essentially the same. The human response to Brainspotting is universal. As past traumas recede, we can experience the present free of their shadows. We can be ourselves in the moment. We can look ahead with curiosity.

The internationalization of Brainspotting is a dream come true for me. The relational aspect of the Dual Attunement Frame is being passed on from person to person and country to country. Therapists are creatively experimenting with Brainspotting every day. I am waiting for someone to have an epiphany equal to or greater to the one I had with Karen, the ice skater. It may happen in the United States, it may happen in Slovenia, or it may happen in a country that doesn't have Brainspotting yet. Nothing stays the same; everything is meant to change. Movement is the human nature and the universal nature. And movement is the nature of the brain.

The Future of Brainspotting

Brainspotting is different from other psychotherapies and healing modalities in a variety of ways. It strategically utilizes the client's visual field to access their brain's self-scanning and self-healing properties. It posits that psychology is a reflection of physiology and that physiological approaches can have psychological consequences. It both intentionally harnesses and intentionally unblocks the human drive for survival and adaptation.

In Brainspotting, it is both acknowledged and embraced that we are working in a field of uncertainty, where we know just a shred of what there is to know about the inner universe of the human brain. Brainspotting therapists know that the only solutions to the problems clients bring to the therapy office lie within the clients themselves. Brainspotting encompasses a full spectrum of possible interventions with clients, according to their needs, from the most activated to the most resourced use of eye position and body experience. It is specifically and intentionally designed to be integrated with other methods.

Finally, Brainspotting completely integrates the therapist's relational and neurobiological attunement to the client. The Brainspotting therapist listens to the client's words and body experience, and observes the eyes, face, and body of the client while watching for reflexive cues. Brainspotting is based on the idea that the human system is self-healing and that the role of the therapist is to set and hold a frame that promotes and utilizes the client's self-healing capacities.

Brainspotting is designed for efficiency. Every session is important, and each session stands on its own. I like to call this concept "wire to wire." This term, which comes from racing and means leading the race from the beginning to the end, reflects the importance of each focused, intentional moment from the beginning of a session through to the end of each session. Laser-like efficiency is possible when you are processing on a Brainspot, as it holds the brain's attention on the precise brain region that needs the healing.

Another unique concept of Brainspotting is that the healing happens not only in the sessions, but also in between the sessions. After all, there are 168 hours in the week, and only one hour is devoted to each session. How can the change possibly occur in such a small fraction of our weekly life? I call this alternate attitude toward time and change in therapy "bookending" because the weekly Brainspotting sessions are seen as bookends on each end of the ongoing processing and change that happens within the client during the week. With this attitude, the Brainspotting sessions, or bookends, are seen as opportunities to facilitate the change that will occur after the session is over. The next, or follow-up, session starts by reviewing and reinforcing the change from the previous week, and then focuses on continuing this change for the coming week, thus providing another bookend.

But what makes Brainspotting truly different from other therapies is that the method itself is designed to be a temporary way station between where the psychotherapy field has come to where it is heading. The breakthroughs accomplished by Brainspotting, as an approach, are not intended to last in the mental health field forever; they are intended to open up new theoretical vistas and clinical discoveries that may ultimately make Brainspotting obsolete. Like a story, everything has a beginning, middle, and an end. The topography of our planet is always in flux, from the outside forces of erosion to the inside pressures of uplift and fracture. The next discovery in psychotherapy, beyond Brainspotting, may happen in the office of a therapist in some far corner of the world, who will have a transcendent experience like the one I had with Karen, the ice skater. Or the next therapeutic breakthrough may happen in a research laboratory or a hospital, as researchers study fMRI (functional magnetic resonance imaging) or QEEG (quantitative electroencephalogram) scans of the brains of people receiving Brainspotting therapy.

Within the context of a research project, a team of brain scientists and I have already conducted a Brainspotting session with a client in an fMRI scanner at a top university hospital in Arkansas. We are studying Brainspotting's effect on the brain of trauma survivors. This first trial yielded promising, yet preliminary results, and we are now looking to conduct additional trials with more subjects. Austrian Brainspotting trainer Thomas Weber is developing a major QEEG and fMRI study of Brainspotting at the most prestigious research hospital in Vienna. Discussions are underway at the University of Pittsburgh School of Medicine to develop a study that will examine how the pupils of the eye respond during Brainspotting sessions. I am excited about the initial results from an international psychological research study comparing the effectiveness of Brainspotting to the effectiveness of EMDR, a study co-conducted by Dr. Mark Stemmler (chairman of the psychology research department at the University of Erlangen, Germany) and me. In Scotland, Dr. Frank Corrigan has written an in-depth journal article speculating on the neurobiological underpinnings of Brainspotting. He believes that Brainspotting directly accesses and heals an area of the brainstem (the area between the parts of the brain called the superior colliculi and the periaqueductal gray, or PAG) that he believes holds "the core self."

• • •

My primary interest and that of others in the growing Brainspotting community is not the power and control issues that seem to arise within virtually all organizational structures. Since the beginning of my career, I have seen well-intended organizations lose their original intentions and unwittingly make self-preservation and expansion their primary goals. In the Brainspotting community, my primary interest is relational; I'm interested in the growing network of relationships between Brainspotting therapists and Brainspotting communities. The relationship is the essential core of both the Brainspotting treatment process between client and therapist, and the growing, global community of Brainspotting therapists. Organizations are important, and each nation where Brainspotting is taught has developed or is developing its own Brainspotting association. However, I am working hard to make sure that Brainspotting doesn't fall into the trap of becoming so structured that the organizations overshadow Brainspotting's relational imperative.

In the future, we hope to bring Brainspotting to new countries in each of the continents where we have already conducted trainings. We are certainly planning to bring Brainspotting to Africa and Asia, where no trainings have occurred as yet.

I am also expanding the learning opportunities for both new and experienced Brainspotting therapists. Although a great deal of time, thought, and development has gone into the basic Phase 1 and 2 trainings, I am continually renewing and upgrading them. In 2011, I added a Phase 3 training for the most advanced Brainspotting therapists; it addresses sports performance and creativity expansion, and includes demonstrations with an athlete and an actor who performs a monologue before and after Brainspotting acting coaching.

The most advanced training I give I named "the Intensive." It is five full days for a maximum of twelve Brainspotting therapists. The designation "intensive" is very accurate, as it is personally challenging for those present. Twelve experiential Brainspotting sessions are conducted in the middle of the group circle; each participant has the opportunity to be the client once and the Brainspotting therapist once. I sit next to the therapist and guide them to work in the most open, creative way, which I call "free-form Brainspotting"—the way I work in my office. In the Intensive, not only is the learning deep, but the personal healing experiences are powerful also. I have conducted fifteen Intensives around the world. My ultimate goal would be to teach Brainspotting on a curriculum basis, the way courses are taught in a university setting. I have found that it is good to expose young therapists to Brainspotting early in their careers, as novices are more open and in need of the Dual Attunement Frame.

• • •

For you, the reader, this book marks the beginning of a Brainspotting journey that is uniquely your own. Perhaps you will seek out and work with a Brainspotting therapist for personal healing or for performance or creativity expansion. No matter what the next step on your journey is, you will take it while being more mindful that "where you look affects how you feel."

Glossary

Please note that some of the words in this glossary are used only in the field of Brainspotting, while others have a more general usage. These general usage terms usually have a specific meaning when used in relation to Brainspotting.

activate (verb) To intentionally intensify our inner emotional and bodily experience by focusing on what is bothering us. We activate in preparation for finding a Brainspot.

activation (noun) A generic, all-encompassing term representing how we perceive the heightening of either emotions or body sensations when we bring our attention to whatever is bothering us.

Activation Eye, the In One-Eye Brainspotting, the eye that, when exposed with the other covered, elicits the higher level of activation. The Activation Eye is used when clients need more focus and/or higher activation.

Activation Model, the The basic model of Brainspotting for clients who can comfortably tolerate higher levels of activation. The Activation Model is in contrast to the Resource Model.

BioLateral Sound Gentle nature sounds and healing music that is programmed to move back and forth from ear to ear. BioLateral Sound, available on CD and as mp3 downloads, is used as background to support the Brainspotting process.

Body Resource, the Where we feel calmest and most grounded in the body. The Body Resource is the foundation of the Resource Model of Brainspotting and is used to find the Resource Brainspot.

Convergence Brainspotting Moving back and forth quickly (every three to ten seconds) between close and far (on the z axis) on a Brainspot. Convergence Brainspotting activates the ocular cardiac reflex (OCR) and leads to rapid, deep processing.

dual attunement The Brainspotting therapist's simulateous attunement to the client's process in the treatment relationship and to the client's brain-body response while on a Brainspot. Dual attunement is the foundation of the Brainspotting process.

Dual Attunement Frame, the The containment provided for the client by the therapist's simultaneous attunement to the relationship and Brainspot. The frame allows the client to effectively use the adaptive nature of their nervous system to locate whatever is unhealed and to resolve it internally.

EMDR Eye movement desensitization and reprocessing, a treatment model developed by Francine Shapiro in the late 1980s. It combines eye movements and other forms of bilateral stimulation with specific protocols and procedures. EMDR is highly researched and used effectively with trauma and other emotional conditions.

Expansion Model, the Uses Brainspotting to promote and enhance performance, creativity, and self-experience. Inherent in the Expansion Model is the belief that human growth potential is infinite.

felt sense, the Coined by Eugene Gendlin, this term refers to something unclear that is felt in the body and also experienced nonverbally.

field of vision, the Also known as the field of view or the visual field, it is the extent of the observable world that can be seen at a given moment. The visual field is where Brainspots are located with the client.

focused activation The state attained by the set-up process of Brainspotting (activation, SUDS level assessment, and body awareness). Focused activation helps the therapist and client to locate the Brainspot and leads to focused mindfulness. It is theorized that activation of the emotions and body sensations that occur around a single issue or situation brings about more focused brain activity.

focused mindfulness The specific form of mindfulness or processing used in Brainspotting, so called because it occurs in the client who is in a state of focused activation, or activated around a specific issue or memory. See also focused activation and processing.

Inside Window Brainspotting The mode of Brainspotting in which the client internally identifies the eye positions with the greatest activation, both horizontally (on the x axis) and vertically (on the y axis).

One-Eye Brainspotting The mode of Brainspotting in which one eye is covered and the other exposed. With one eye, the client feels the greatest level of activation (the Activation Eye), and with the other, the greatest level of calm groundedness (the Resource Eye). Once the difference is determined, the Brainspotting therapist can guide the client to use the most appropriate eye for processing, according to the client's unique needs of the moment.

Outside Window Brainspotting The original mode of Brainspotting in which the therapist locates and uses eye positions by observing reflexive responses in the client's eyes, face, or body.

Parasympathetic Processing Processing that is performed while the parasympathetic (calming) nervous system is simultaneously activated. Parasymapathetic Processing is used in the Resource Model of Brainspotting with highly vulnerable and dissociated clients.

performance trauma A trauma experienced during practice for a performance or during a performance itself. Such trauma can include physical injuries, failures, and humiliations. Performance traumas accumulate in the nervous system of the performer from childhood and ultimately lead to performance blocks and anxiety.

process (verb) To emotionally and/or neurobiologically experience, internally, step-by-step, over a proscribed period of time, in order to affect a change of perception or attitude.

processing (noun) A client's internal experience, including memories, thoughts, emotions, or sensations in their body, as observed by the client, step-by-step, over a proscribed period of time. In Brainspotting, this processing is done in a state of focused activation and is thus referred to as focused mindfulness.

Resource Brainspot See the Resource Spot.

Resource Eye, the In One-Eye Brainspotting, the eye that, when exposed with the other covered, elicits the lower level of activation. The Resource Eye is used when clients need more containment and/ or lower activation.

Resource Spot, the The Brainspot that matches the Body Resource (where we feel calmest and most grounded in the body).

somatic experiencing (SE) A method of accessing and tracking the resources of the body to help heal trauma. Developed by Peter Levine, SE uses pendulating, or moving back and forth, between the areas of strength (the healing vortex) and vulnerability (the trauma vortex) to help the nervous system complete the frozen trauma and to heal.

sports trauma See performance trauma.

Suggested Resources

WORKS REFERENCED IN THIS BOOK

Badenoch, Bonnie. *Being a Brain-Wise Therapist: A Practical Guide to Interpersonal Neurobiology.* New York: W. W. Norton & Company, 2008.

Bergmann, Uri. *Neurobiological Foundations for EMDR Practice.* New York: Springer Publishing Company, 2012.

Doidge, Norman. *The Brain That Changes Itself: Stories of Personal Triumph from the Frontiers of Brain Science.* New York: Penguin Books, 2007.

Grand, David. *Emotional Healing at Warp Speed: The Power of EMDR.* New York, NY: Harmony, 2001.

Grand, David and Alan Goldberg. *This Is Your Brain on Sports: Beating Blocks, Slumps and Performance Anxiety for Good!* Indianapolis: Dog Ear Publishing, 2011.

Martinez-Conde, Susana, and Stephen L. Macknik. "Windows on the Mind." *Scientific American,* 297 no. 2 (August 2007): 56–63.

Scaer, Robert. *The Body Bears the Burden: Trauma, Dissociation, and Disease.* New York: Routledge, 2007.

Scaer, Robert. *The Trauma Spectrum: Hidden Wounds and Human Resiliency.* New York: W. W. Norton & Company, 2005.

Siegel, Daniel. *Pocket Guide to Interpersonal Neurobiology: An Integrative Handbook of the Mind.* New York: W. W. Norton & Company, 2012.

Schiffer, Fredric. *Of Two Minds: A New Approach For Better Understanding and Improving Your Emotional Life.* London: Pocket Books, 1997.

HOW TO FIND A BRAINSPOTTING THERAPIST

To find a Brainspotting therapist in the United States, please go to brainspottingdirectory.com. If you are interested in finding a Brainspotting therapist outside the United States, please go to the website Brainspotting International (brainspottinginternational.org), and click on "Global BSPI Network" (or go directly to brainspottinginternational.org/global-bsp-organizations) for links to Brainspotting organizations around the world.

GENERAL INFORMATION

Brainspotting.com is the official website for David Grand, PhD. This site provides comprehensive information about Brainspotting in the United States and around the world. It includes videos of David Grand and Robert Scaer talking about Brainspotting, and an "inside view" of Brainspotting written by a client.

BioLateral.com provides information on purchasing CDs and downloading mp3s of BioLateral Sound, Brainspotting Phase 1 and 2 DVD trainings, and articles and an audio on David Grand's work with New York Mets catcher Mackey Sasser.

Brainspottinginternational.org provides information about Brainspotting organizations in Europe, the Middle East, South America, and Australia. See the site's "Global BSP Organizations" page for contact information and links to each organization.

Acknowledgments

My deepest thanks to the Sounds True family for supporting me in making this book a reality. Thank you to Tami Simon for believing that *Brainspotting* was worthy of publishing and for supporting me throughout the creative process. Deep appreciation to my editor, Amy Rost, for countless hours of helping me shape the book into a fluent, cohesive form. Her patience and skill made for excellent collaboration that at times was even fun. Thanks to Jennifer Holder for picking up the strand of a final edit and bringing the book to completion.

Thanks are due to my assistant, Laurie Delaney, who supported my efforts with the competence, dedication, loyalty, and good cheer she brings to everything she does.

Special thanks to Pie Frey who has selflessly promoted Brainspotting and made the Rocky Mountain region of Colorado a bastion for it. Deep appreciation to Esly Carvalho for first bringing Brainspotting to Brazil and then to Ecuador, Portugal, and Spain. Thanks to Mario Salvador for his gifts in developing Brainspotting in Spain and then bringing it to Romania, Slovenia, and Bosnia. Warm appreciation to Fran Yoeli for bringing Brainspotting to Israel and supporting its growth in Greece with Tessa Pratos. Thank you to Glenda Villamarin and Santiago Jacome for Brainspotting work in Ecuador and Chile. Appreciation to Maria Elena Aduriz for opening Argentina and South America to me. Thanks to Philip Dutton and Marie-Jose Boon for bringing Brainspotting to the United Kingdom and the Netherlands.

Thank you to my all my Brainspotting trainers for their dedication, including in the United States: Roberto Weisz, Ruby Gibson, and Margot Nacey. Internationally: Margarida Cuoto and Luciana Caruso.

Deep thanks to Robert Scaer for his personal and professional support. Appreciation to Norman Doidge for his valued support. Thank you to Uri Bergmann for his friendship and for teaching me everything I know about the brain. Gratitude to Chaya Kaufmann for teaching me the true meaning of the word "courage." Appreciation to Mark Stemmler for his stalwart work on the foundational research for Brainspotting. Thank you to Frank Corrigan for his studies on the neurobiology of Brainspotting. Thanks to Rob Polishook and Alan Goldman for help with developing the Sports Trauma Model. Thanks to my Brainspotting family, which includes Christine Ranck, Martha Jacobi, Cynthia Schwartzberg, Deborah Antinori, Susan Pinco, Alecia Ralston, Tom Taylor, Susan Dowell, Russ Camarda, Sjoerd DeJongh, Terrie Williams, Elyse Kirsch, Laura Hillesheim, Earl Poteet, Annette Goodman, Sylvia Guz, Andre Monteiro, Calder Kaufmann, Diane Israel, Iria Salvador, Connie Konikoff, Petra Riedel, Erika Thorkildsen, and Barbro Andersen.

Most loving thanks to my wife, Nina, who has been through everything with me—including countless hours at the dining room table writing and editing this book. Love to my son, Jonathan, for his humor and inspiration, culled from all he has survived. Thank you to my father for the literal and figurative pointer that guides my way.

About the Author

David Grand, a licensed clinical social worker with a PhD from International University, maintains a private psychotherapy practice in Manhattan. His client roster includes many successful television, film, and stage actors; professional athletes; business leaders; survivors of profound traumas (including 9/11 and Hurricane Katrina); and Iraq and Afghanistan combat veterans. He now spends several months every year traveling around the world, lecturing and training therapists on the use of Brainspotting. He is the author of *Emotional Healing at Warp Speed* (Harmony, 2001), the director and producer of the documentary film *Come Hell or High Water,* and the playwright of *I Witness.* He has been interviewed on CNN, NBC, *Nightline,* the *Jane Pauley Show,* and *NBC Extra,* and featured in the *New York Times,* the *Washington Post, O Magazine, Golf Digest,* and *Newsday.* For more information, please visit brainspotting.com.

About Sounds True

Sounds True is a multimedia publisher whose mission is to inspire and support personal transformation and spiritual awakening. Founded in 1985 and located in Boulder, Colorado, we work with many of the leading spiritual teachers, thinkers, healers, and visionary artists of our time. We strive with every title to preserve the essential "living wisdom" of the author or artist. It is our goal to create products that not only provide information to a reader or listener, but that also embody the quality of a wisdom transmission.

For those seeking genuine transformation, Sounds True is your trusted partner. At SoundsTrue.com you will find a wealth of free resources to support your journey, including exclusive weekly audio interviews, free downloads, interactive learning tools, and other special savings on all our titles. To listen to a podcast interview with Sounds True publisher Tami Simon and author David Grand, visit SoundsTrue.com/bonus/Brainspotting.